Musings of a Horse Farm Corgi

Leslie McDonald

Foreword by Mary Phelps

ISBN: 0615638341
ISBN-13: 9780615638348

Down the Aisle Promotions

Photo Credit – Doug Froh

Other Titles by
Leslie McDonald

Down the Aisle

Published by Down the Aisle Promotions

Making Magic

Published by Half Halt Press,

co-written with Meredith Weller, DVM

Tic-Tac

Published by Dodd, Mead & Company

under maiden name of Leslie McDonald

To Trish . . .

thanks for that special inspiration
that grows from friendship.

Foreword

My Corgis have always been a large part of the magic of my life. From their Welsh legends as the carriers of the woodland fairies, to the Queen's obsession, I had wanted as long as I could remember to have Corgis in my life. I am on the second generation now, Tasha (named by my mother after the famed illustrator and Corgi lover Tasha Tudor) and Trooper (named because he is my protector and barks deeply when the word "patrol" is uttered) are almost always by my side. When I have to travel without them, they are welcome guests in friend's home so they can get their "Corgi fix".

They were preceded by Winnie, my first love, and then Gizmo, who waited until I returned from The World Cup Final in the Netherlands to deliver her first litter; a girl and a boy, named after the first and second placed winners that year, Anky (Van Grunsven) and Sven (Rothenberger). Gizmo's second litter was distributed across the dressage world. All now romping beyond the Rainbow Bridge and will no doubt greet me en-mass when it is my time to cross over to the universe.

We have conversations all the time. They make me smile in the morning, lick my tears when I am sad, and stay close by, letting me know I will always be loved and appreciated. Whenever I see another Corgi at a show, I have to stop and touch, sharing the same favors when my short-legged assistants accompany me in my travels.

When I was able to finally fulfill a lifelong dream of at last owning a pony and doing combined driving, I had the carriage maker design a special box for my single seated marathon vehicle so Tasha could keep me company. She has come along through miles of woodland trails, been by my side training at a gallop through water obstacles, and sat vigilantly in my show carriage during my first pleasure show "Carriage Dog" class. We won it, and later that day the judge confessed, "there was no question in my mind which dog would get the blue ribbon."

Corgis … they capture your heart and fill your life with incomparable joy. *Musings of a Horse Farm Corgi* is a peek into the world of an engaging Corgi named Beamer who shares a view of life from his unique perspective. He is definitely a dynamic little fellow who Tasha and I have enjoyed befriending on these pages.

Mary Phelps
www.horsesdaily.com
www.dressagedaily.com

Introduction

I've always admired Corgis for that special brand of cocky character with which they take on the world. There is no end to the exuberant entertainment provided by these sturdy little fellows as they confidently strut their stuff.

I didn't have the opportunity to invite a Corgi into my life until the day Beamer came along. He followed a much loved parade of Cockers, Westies, Malamutes, Goldens, Labs and even a wolf hybrid who each carved their personal niche at my horse farm. Every one of them won a special place in my heart, but it wasn't until Beamer that I knew without a doubt that I had finally met my canine soul mate.

From day one, Beamer never failed to assert his very strong personality over everyone who made his acquaintance. From his unique perspective, he had no shortage of opinions on everything from visitors to entertainment to playtime and his never ending quest for food.

Even though I'd like to take the credit for *Musings of a Horse Farm Corgi,* I'm fairly certain that Beamer is responsible for planting the seed of inspiration in my imagination from which his story unfolded onto these pages. During the writing of his book, Beamer never failed to station himself at my side whenever and wherever I was working on the manuscript. Although his independent nature could sometimes make him seem aloof, when it came to his book, he never missed a pen stroke.

Without a doubt, I sensed he was overseeing my work to be sure I told his story accurately. Whenever I looked down at him for inspiration, I'd find him looking back up at me with an engaging tilt of his head, encouraging me to find just the right words. I've always thought that unique expression was the doorway into his special view of life. No author could ask for a better muse than my little buddy. Thanks, Beamer, for inviting me into your world.

CHAPTER
ONE

Beginnings

We all have the same beginnings, entering the world with our unique flaws and foibles. Fresh souls brimming over with unsullied promise are launched on our future path, guided by a dose of luck or perhaps a preordained script. With a cry, a nicker, a mew, a chirp, or (in my case) a yip, we announce our arrival into the bright unknown.

On May 16, 1999, on the west side of Cincinnati, my littermates and I slid from the dark, warm security of our mother's womb. We were five newborn corgis, wiggling and squiggling against the soft belly of our mother, Rosemary, as she sought to nurture and direct us in those formative days with a tender nuzzle or a corrective nip. A cluster of pups, three girls and two boys, made it hard to tell where each of us started or ended.

A show ring champion under her formal name of Hapusbyrn's Tri to Remember, Rosemary was now three litters away from the competition ring, focused on what she considered to be a much more satisfying career. She was proud of her healthy new batch of pups. According to ancient legend, corgis were the enchanted mounts of the woodland fairy warriors. White shoulder markings still bore the harness outline of the fairy saddles, while newborn floppy ears that would soon stand up in jaunty attention had served as handles for their tiny riders to grasp as they rode into battle. A proud legacy for her pups to live up to.

I came into the world inheriting the legacy and markings of my Corgi ancestors who had proudly carried the woodland fairy warriors into battle.

We were all little Hapusbyrns, initially known only by the name of our home kennel which translated to Happy Hill in Welsh. Official monikers would have to wait until we caught the eye of a prospective buyer wanting a special corgi pup to fill a void in his or her heart. My first identifying title was AKC#DL789768, and I was known informally around our kennel as Hapusbyrn puppy number five. Certainly not a name to cause a puppy to trip over his paws in response when called!

However, in those early days, names didn't matter much. My sole focus was on Rosemary, who easily identified us by a simple yip or a nip. It was an effective communication system, since the five of us tended to respond en masse to satisfy our simple, basic needs for food or nurturing. But, believe me; whenever one of us deserved individual correction, we knew exactly to whom her yip was directed.

After a few weeks, tiny sparks of personality began to glimmer, setting us apart as individuals. Curiosity gradually drew us out of the puppy pile. Hesitantly at first, we only ventured a few feet before tumbling back to the security of Rosemary's nest. But, in time, the feet became yards, until we were independently sniffing the wire perimeter of the puppy pen or poking curiously at the little plush toys and balls tossed in for our entertainment.

From the earliest days, we had been attended by a large woman who appeared several times a day, seemingly from a hole in the ceiling. Her entrance was announced by a rhythmic thumping as she descended a wooden staircase into our room. Rosemary was always overjoyed to see her.

Every day, after first greeting and feeding Rosemary, the woman would carefully examine each of us pups. Her big, gentle hands would inspect under tails, pry open mouths, and gently prod round little bellies. We were even weighed regularly on a small scale. Once satisfied that all was in order, she would return up the stairs that disappeared into an unknown world above the ceiling.

As the days progressed, my thoughts began to expand beyond the scope of the puppy pile where my siblings were still happily ensconced. Although Rosemary remained the central orb in my universe, I was beginning to realize that there was much more to experience than the furry realm of her underbelly. What was on the other side of the wire mesh fence that surrounded our basement pen? No matter how I prodded and pawed, there was only enough room between the link sections to poke the tip of my nose through to the other side.

And, who was the woman that visited us several times a day to tend to our needs? She certainly didn't smell like a puppy—or like Rosemary, for that matter—who seemed bowled over with excitement when the woman called her name. She wiggled and whimpered with the delight of a puppy whenever the woman stroked her glossy tricolored coat.

So, what was a pup's relationship to be with this very different creature that walked on two legs? Since she was obviously someone important to our existence. I determined it was to my advantage to show her extra affection whenever she visited our pen. To my delight, my efforts were rewarded with a loving dose of attention that far exceeded that given to my littermates.

Five weeks after we were born, a new woman thumped down the steps behind our caregiver. One by one, she carefully inspected us from head to toe, admiring each pup's attributes. I was the last to be checked. As our caretaker handed me over, the corners of her mouth turned down in an expression that I had never seen before. Usually she cuddled me with a big smile while spouting silly, high-pitched puppy gibberish. This unexpected sadness worried me.

There was definite concern in the visitor's voice. "It's always hard to tell at this age, but I think you're right. He does look like he's going to be a fluffy. That means definitely no show career or breeding in his future. You'll have to inform any buyers who might be interested so they know what they're getting into."

With that, I was gently replaced in the pen as they sadly shook their heads. I yipped loudly to get their attention. *Fluffy? Wait! What does **that** mean?*

For the first time, the visiting woman smiled down at me when my yips grew more frantic. "How cute. The little guy doesn't seem to want us to leave. Looks like he's a real people puppy. At least he's got that going for him."

I stood a little separate from my littermates, watching in bewilderment as the women disappeared up the stairs. In a word, they had proclaimed I was different, but how? I just couldn't see it, but somehow I felt that their simple pronouncement of *fluffy* had just changed my life. Only the day before, I had been a contented member of a litter of five nursing, playing, and growing pups born in the same mold. We looked and acted alike. All our parts were in perfect working order, but suddenly I had been differentiated by the unexplained stigma of being "a fluffy."

Not wanting my littermates to realize that I was somehow different, I waited until they were fast asleep for their afternoon nap before taking my mother aside. She gently licked my head, trying to calm the worry as I related how the visitor had marked me with the unexplained curse of the fluffy.

Rosemary was bewildered, without any idea of what *fluffy* meant. To her, all the puppies were perfect little souls destined for loving homes and even the show ring, just like her previous litters. She tried to console me with stories of how she was certain that a special mistress was waiting to select me, just as she had been chosen from her litter by our caretaker five years earlier. Someday very soon, she explained, potential owners would begin to visit us in search of an ideal puppy to make their home complete.

She guaranteed that, while I would feel sad at first to leave her and my siblings, a special new life with my very own personal human awaited, just beyond the perimeter of the puppy pen. In her mind, there was no doubt that I was extremely desirable because I was a tricolor male from top bloodlines. In fact, since I was the only tricolor in the litter, it set me apart in a special way. She couldn't imagine any reason why I wouldn't be valued as highly as my siblings.

Rosemary gave my little round bottom a confident nudge toward my littermates. Still uncertain, but somewhat pacified, I curled up to join the napping puppy pile, but the unexplained specter of the fluffy made my sleep fitful.

I was still fretting over the worrisome fluffy label when, a few days later, our caretaker brought a new visitor down the steps. "I'm happy to show you the pups, but just remember they're still too young to leave their mother. They won't be ready to go for three more weeks."

I couldn't see the visitor yet, but the voice that responded was younger, with a barely concealed edge of excitement. "Thanks so much for giving me an early peek at your puppies. I've been searching for a tricolor male for several months, but just haven't found the right one."

My ears immediately perked up. *Tricolor? Male? Hey, that's me!*

I quickly cut out of the puppy pile before the women's feet hit the bottom step, determined to charm our visitor before she had a chance to notice my siblings. When she came into view, I was already in position, looking up with an adorable cock of my head that I had mastered to garner extra praise from our caretaker.

It worked! The moment the visitor saw me, she dropped to her knees on the other side of the pen, scrunching down so we were eye to eye. I noticed she had a warm smile and friendly green eyes that searched my face.

I poked my little nose through the fence, licking her extended fingers. *Careful,* I warned myself, slowing down my tongue action. *You want to charm her with cute, but don't overdo it.*

"What a precious little man," she exclaimed. "Look how he's so brave to leave the other puppies to come meet me. He's just perfect."

"He is a darling," our caretaker agreed. "In fact, he's got the best personality of the bunch, but there's something I need to tell you before you fall in love and make a decision."

I caught my breath. "Yip...yip...YIP!" I barked, frantically jumping against the fence to distract the visitor. But, it was too late; the dreaded curse of the fluffy was about to be revealed.

"Unfortunately, this cute little fellow is what we breeders call a "fluffy," our caretaker explained, as I desperately increased my licking of the visitor's fingers, hoping to redirect her attention. "That means he has a genetic coat mutation that will ultimately result in a long fluffy coat, as opposed to the normal short, stiff corgi coat."

The visitor withdrew her fingers, looking up at the other woman with concern. "What exactly does that mean for this puppy?"

Our caretaker gave me a sad little frown. "It's considered a conformation flaw that would be severely punished in the show ring. As a result, he can't be shown and should never be used for breeding. However, he could still compete in performance events like obedience or agility. Some people find them very cute and cuddly because of the coat, but they're definitely not up to the breed standard."

I sat back on my haunches, letting out a long breath as the revelation of the curse sank in. *That's it? My coat's the problem? But, I don't look any different from my brother and sisters. What's all the fuss?*

"The coat flaw isn't obvious at this young age," the caretaker continued, as though reading my mind. "But, gradually he'll develop a long silky coat, which is unacceptable for a herding breed. The soft hair is not water-resistant, so it makes these dogs unsuitable for farm work. The texture mats easily, collecting burrs and dirt, and requires too much grooming to maintain as a working farm dog. A normal corgi's coat is coarse and water-resistant. It doesn't mat or retain dirt.

"Hard as it is to believe when you look at this cute little fellow," she continued, "in the old days, Welsh farmers would destroy any fluffies, as the coat made them unfit for work.

However, today, on the rare occasion that one shows up in a litter, we sell them at a reduced price as pet quality."

The visitor thoughtfully reached over the fence and carefully picked me up. She held me very gently in the palms of her hands, brushing my coat with her cheek. Her breath was light against my ear tips, and her touch was so tender that I felt as safe and secure as when Rosemary snuggled me.

"Well, little man, I think you're just wonderful, no matter what she says about your coat," she whispered softly into my fur. "Showing or breeding is not important to me. First and foremost, I'm looking for a good companion, and you seem to fit the bill. How could I ever find a more independent, affectionate puppy?"

"Before you make a final decision, here's a suggestion," our caretaker offered. "Since this puppy is too young for you to take today, let me give you some literature on fluffies, including pictures, so you can see what the adults look like. Right now you're thinking with your heart because he's so cute and obviously likes you. Take the next few weeks to make an educated decision. I want you to end up with the corgi you had in mind when you started your search. Since this little fellow is not going to be up to type, I don't want you to be unhappy about your choice when his fluffy coat starts to appear in a few months."

The visitor studied me carefully before setting me gently back in the pen with an uncertain pat. "He just seems so perfect, but maybe you're right. I should probably take the time to study all the information."

After a hesitant smile in my direction, she followed our caretaker up the stairs without looking back.

I didn't move for a long time, watching the stairs where she had disappeared. Hope slowly dwindled as I realized that she wasn't returning. I sank down with my head on my paws next to the fence where she had held me. The sweet floral scent of her perfume still lingered in her absence.

I was certain that I had just been held by the special human that Rosemary had promised was destined to claim me for her own. But, just as quickly as she had appeared, it seemed she had been frightened away by the threat of the fluffy curse. Would she ever return, or would I be left behind in the puppy pen as my more perfect brothers and sisters found loving homes with their own special humans?

As the days progressed, my littermates and I quickly grew in stature and stamina. However, while they seemed to flourish, my usually perky light began to dim. Rosemary was frustrated by her inability to cheer me. Even our caretaker grew concerned when I ceased to trot over to greet her with a jaunty tilt of my head. I, who had always been the first to the fence to meet her, was now bowled over by my siblings as I hung at the back of the pen.

Our caretaker began spending extra time on my daily physical exams, trying to discern a cause for the unexplained reversal in my condition. "What's happened to my happy little man? There's no sign that you're sick, but you seem to be fading away from me."

I'd give her a long, soulful gaze in appreciation for her concern, but how could I explain that the curse of the fluffy had stripped me of my hopes, as well as my confidence, as first one sister and then my only brother were adopted by loving owners who never gave me a second look. I sensed it was only a matter of time until I would be left alone with Rosemary, who would soon be focused on creating a new litter of puppies to fill the pen.

As my littermates and I grew bigger and stronger, our world began to expand beyond the perimeter of our basement pen. It wasn't long before we were treated to sunny outings in a small grassy yard behind the house.

On a warm afternoon at the end of June as Rosemary, my two remaining sisters, and I were dozing in the fenced backyard, a white pickup truck pulled into the driveway. My mother and the girls trotted over to the gate to greet the visitor while I hung back in the cool shade of the azalea bush. As it seemed that most potential puppy customers were not interested in me because of the fluffy curse, I could see no reason to put on a show for them.

I kept my eyes closed to the soft breeze, trying to tune out the excited squeals of my sisters. But just then, through their yips, I thought I recognized a voice that I had never expected to hear again. "Hey, little man. Are you ready to go home with me?"

I squeezed my eyes shut tighter, certain that my imagination was playing cruel games. It couldn't be. Or, maybe, just maybe, could it really be her?

And then, I smelled it; a sweet floral perfume that had been a fading hope in my memory for the past three weeks. In that moment, I knew it was OK to open my eyes.

CHAPTER
TWO

Respect

My sisters and I wiggled and pounced happily around the visitor's feet, encouraged by her laughter at our antics. My siblings weren't certain of the cause for my excitement as we bowled each other over in joyous puppy abandon, but it didn't matter to them, since corgis never needed an excuse to celebrate.

However, Rosemary sagely knew the visitor's purpose as soon as she had entered our yard. My mother watched us frolic from her station beside our caretaker, a little sad, but grateful that my uncertain future finally seemed to have been secured by what appeared to be a perfectly acceptable human. When our excitement ramped down, Rosemary covered my face and ear tips with lingering good-bye licks to let me know I would always have a special place in her heart.

My caretaker swept me into her arms, holding me close to her ample chest as she had done every day of my young life. She stroked me gently, a big smile replacing the concern her face had worn the past few weeks.

"On your way, little man," she whispered, her cheek brushing the soft fur on my head. "There's a big world waiting out there. I have a good feeling that you're going to master it handily."

As I looked down at Rosemary and my siblings huddled at my caretaker's feet, the finality of her words gave pause to my excitement. No matter how long I had dreamed of and hoped for this day, the inescapable curse of the fluffy hadn't let me believe it would actually come to pass.

Rosemary was staring up at me with soulful eyes beside my sisters, who for once were quiet, as though even they recognized the magnitude of the moment. As much as Rosemary had prepared all of us pups for moving-on day, I suddenly realized that, excited as I was to begin a new life with my very own special human, I would probably never again see this family that had been the center of my universe since birth.

My caretaker broke the moment by carefully placing me in a blue plastic dog carrier with a wire door. The bottom was covered by a gray fleece blanket topped by a new plush bunny toy that still smelled like the store packaging. Rosemary and my sisters crowded around the door to exchange one last nose touch.

The transaction was officially completed when my new mistress picked up the carrier and took it to her big white truck. After shaking hands with my caretaker, she securely strapped my carrier into the passenger seat. I gave her fingers a little lick through the grate when she snapped the seat belt across the wire door.

Her eyes melted into an even bigger smile as they met mine. "Hey, little man, it's great to have you on board. Hang in there. It won't be long until I get you home to meet the whole family."

Family? That'll be fun, I thought, imagining a house full of playful children just waiting to meet the new puppy. I didn't know where we were going, but I couldn't wait to find out. All I knew was that I was on my way to a new future with my very own special human, whose love for me had been strong enough to overcome the fluffy curse.

We were off with the roar of the diesel engine. As we pulled out of the driveway, my new mistress clicked on the radio. Strains of "Respect" belted from the speaker, sung by a woman with real, gritty soul in her voice. *Now there's a great theme song for the start of my new life,* I decided, twitching my nose to the beat.

I curled up in a corner of my carrier, looking up through the door grate to really study my new mistress for the first time. Although she was intent on driving, occasionally she would smile down at the crate, taking a hand off the wheel to reach across the seat and let me lick her fingers through the wire. She was much younger than my caretaker, but had the same type of friendly face. Her brown hair was in a ponytail that poked out through the back of a navy baseball cap.

"First order of business is to give you a real name," she declared, as my tongue played with her thumbnail. "The moment I met you, it was like being warmed by a sunbeam. I'd never seen such a happy, bright puppy. So, I decided that just has to be your name: Beamer. It's a perfect fit because you'll always be my little sunbeam."

Beamer? I cocked my head thoughtfully. *Short and to the point. I like it!*

In that moment of truck-seat christening, AKC#DL789768, aka Hapusbyrn puppy number five, officially became Beamer. As the new name began to settle over me, I felt the curse of the fluffy recede a little farther into the background.

Now that I had an official name and a new permanent relationship, it seemed totally inappropriate that the carrier should divide us on this very special day. Being restrained in a plastic box on a truck seat was not how I envisioned my new life should begin. It was definitely time for me to take a cue from the "Respect" song on the radio and take charge of the situation.

Tentatively, I made a first test of my powers of canine control, emitting a sad yet slightly pleading, "Whimper... whimper...whimper."

My new mistress's eyes remained straight ahead on the road, without any acknowledgment, as she passed a truck.

Undeterred, and motivated with renewed determination, I ramped up my plea with a more pathetic, insistent, "Whimper…whimper…yip…YIP!"

She flashed me a concerned frown. *Gotcha!* I declared in triumphant satisfaction, as she returned her fingers to the carrier for me to lick.

"It's OK, little man," she cooed to soothe me. "I know how you must miss your family, but I promise you're going to love your new life. We've got such adventures waiting. Once you're grown up, you're going to be the Corgi in Charge at my horse farm."

Horse? I had absolutely no idea what she meant. Rosemary had coached us pups on potential home prospects, but she had never mentioned anything about horses. There had been discussions about the variety of breeds we would meet at dog shows and agility trials. We had even been educated about children who would make the best playmates. But horses? I just couldn't imagine what my new owner had in mind.

"It's a big responsibility," she continued. "We have a very busy barn at home. There will be students to greet and horses to oversee, but I know you'll be up to it. I knew you were the perfect fellow for the job the first time we met. It was just luck that I found you."

She thinks she's the lucky one? I thought with amazement, remembering how, during our first meeting, I had thrown myself at her with a load of adorable before she had a chance to even notice my brother and sisters.

Definitely not satisfied with fingers alone, more than ever I craved complete contact with this special human who was mine alone. I'd waited too long for this moment to be separated by the wire door of this cage. Nothing to do but throw back my head and let loose the most pitiful, heartbreaking howl I could conjure up from my innermost puppy.

Seriously concerned, my new mistress steered the truck to a stop on the shoulder of the road. "You sound so unhappy, my poor little man. Mrs. Carpenter said I should keep you in the carrier on the way home, but that cry is just too sad to keep you locked up. C'mon over here, Beamer. You can ride the rest of the way in my lap. Maybe that will help you miss your family a little less."

Bingo! As quick as you could say, "Wham, bam, thank you, ma'am," I was carefully lifted out of that restrictive little crate. She held me to her cheek, rubbing her nose in my fur. When I licked her hand, she placed me softly in her lap, where I snuggled happily into the warm corduroy of her pants.

I sighed with the satisfaction of a mission successfully completed as she gently scratched me behind my little ears. *Watch out, world. There's a puppy in charge that just won the corgi lottery and is looking for a little R-E-S-P-E-C-T!*

CHAPTER
THREE

The Farm

Late afternoon, when the truck pulled into the farm's stable yard, I was fast asleep, puffing little puppy snores into my new owner's lap. Totally exhausted from the morning's overwhelming excitement, it took my mistress a few moments of gentle scratching behind my ears to wake me. I blinked hard, trying to grasp the reality of where I was. Only a few brief hours earlier, I had been eating breakfast kibbles with my littermates at my old caretaker's home, totally ignorant of all the life-changing events that were to occur this day.

"Hey, wake up, Beamer," my new owner encouraged. "Welcome to your new home, little man."

My nose twitched with sleepy contentment. *Home? How great does that sound?*

After a good long stretch on her lap, it was time to check things out. I perched on my hind legs, front paws on the door armrest, to peer curiously out the driver's side window to see for myself. It was a good thing her hand supported my pudgy puppy belly; otherwise, I would have toppled over from astonishment at the sight that stretched before me.

The view was unlike anything I had ever experienced at my birth home. The first eight weeks of life had passed simply in our basement puppy pen, with its familiar plush toys and cuddly flannel blanket strips. After four weeks, we had been treated to daily supervised outings in the small fenced yard with a big shade tree behind the little white ranch house where we had been born. It was the best location for long naps following roaring rips with my littermates around the grassy perimeter, tumbling over each other in the pursuit of butterflies.

However, the current view out the truck window far exceeded any potential lifestyle Rosemary had described as possible, even in my most imaginative dreams. Before me stood an oversized world that definitely appeared to lack any of the secure puppy boundaries in which my short-lived life had been anchored.

Immediately in front of the truck was a large gray barn with two big sliding doors, open to reveal an aisle too long to see the end of from my vantage point. *Much too big to be a kennel*, I puzzled, *but it doesn't look like a house. What could possibly need so much space?*

Beside the barn, stretching far back into the prop-erty, were grassy fields, sectioned off by four board fences. Within the pastures grazed creatures bigger than any I had ever imagined existed. They stood on four legs just like a dog, but were so tall that I was certain a full-sized corgi wouldn't even come up to their knees. They had pretty heads on long necks that stretched down to eat the grass, which I had never before considered a food source. On their rumps hung long, luxurious tails that continuously swished while they grazed.

Unable to take my eyes off them, I wondered what on earth the giant beasts could be. Suddenly, without warning, a large brown one bolted across his paddock, bucking and snorting, digging up chunks of turf with his hooves. I jerked nervously against my mistress's stomach as the beast threw back his head, emitting an ear-piercing squeal.

"Don't worry, Beamer," she laughed, giving my bottom a reassuring pat. "That's just Anders celebrating your arrival. He's my big gun in the show ring. I know you'll come to love him and all the other horses that live on our farm. But, just remember to love them from afar. Your first farm lesson is to never, ever chase a horse. No matter how much it looks like fun when they run or buck in the field, it's way too dangerous a game for dogs to play."

I wanted to reassure her that there was nothing tempt-ing about the giant, snorting creature that would entice me to chase it, but at that moment I was distracted by a stout black cat with four white paws. She strolled out of the barn with an arrogant swagger as though she owned the place. Pausing for a moment to take in the truck, she focused on me, her amber eyes locking with mine. Absently, she lifted a front paw, slowly licking it claw by claw by claw. Certain that my full attention was captured, she casually disappeared around the corner of the stable, punctuating her exit with a flick of her tail's white tip.

My mistress noticed my curious shift in attention from the pasture. "That's Spats. She's our barn kitty. Great mouser, but not in the least bit dog friendly. Best to give her a wide berth, at least until you're big enough that she doesn't outweigh you. And even then, I'd be on good behavior around her. Definitely not a kitty for chasing."

I readily agreed, remembering Rosemary's early lessons pertaining to canine/feline relationships. She had emphasized there were two types of cats: those to be chased for sport, and those to be avoided at all costs in the interest of personal health and well-being. According to my new owner, Spats clearly fit into the latter category, advice to be remembered rather than learned the hard way.

"WOOF! WOOF! WOOF!" A loud, harmonious duet resonated from the barn aisle, breaking my thoughts of Spats, as a pair of Labrador retrievers came charging toward the truck, thick tails wagging in joyous greeting. One was black and the other yellow, but except for the color they were identical twins in appearance and behavior. They stood shoulder to shoulder, big front paws perched on the truck's running board, wiggling with excitement over our arrival.

I wasn't certain about Elsa and Audrey's enthusiastic welcome as they eagerly crowded beside the truck to make my acquaintance.

I looked down in disbelief at the fat, wet noses pushing eagerly mere inches from me. I pressed back harder into my mistress's chest, unable to imagine what new horror would appear next. I couldn't conceive of how I would ever conjure up the courage necessary to hold my own in this very foreign environment. Giant squealing horses? Cantankerous cats? And now, oversized wiggling dogs? How was I ever to make my way in this new world that was to be my home?

Sensing my uneasiness, my mistress gently ruffled my coat. "Beamer, meet Elsa and Audrey. Elsa is the yellow Lab and Audrey's mother. They're really good girls who are quite inseparable. They live in the stable and watch over the property. The Labbies are fine for play," she assured me, "but you should probably wait to do any chasing with them until you're big enough to hold your own. Otherwise, they just might bowl you over."

I was just trying to grasp the concept of a playful relationship with the big, boisterous Labbies when a rousing shout from the brick ranch house across the driveway distracted me. "You're home! Let's see our new little man. I've been waiting all morning to meet him."

A large balding man with a fringe of red hair hurried toward us, tilting his head to try and see into the cab of the truck. "Beeeaaammmerrr," he said, drawing out my name with the same high-pitched puppy chatter used by so many of the prospective buyers who had visited my caretaker's home.

"That's my husband," my mistress explained, rolling down the window to allow for a better view. "He's a real puppy lover. You're going to be just as special to him as you are to me."

Before I could turn my full attention to the man approaching the truck, a car drove into the stable yard, horn honking and arms waving out both open windows.

"Did you get the puppy? Where is he? We want to be the first to meet him!"

My mistress held me up for inspection as the car drove past to park in front of the stable. "That's Janice and Diane. They're riding students of mine who board their horses with us. You'll be seeing a lot of them. They love dogs almost as much as their horses. Just don't let them spoil you with those treats they keep in their tack boxes. I'm sure that's why the Labbies are so pudgy."

She reached for the door handle. "C'mon, Beamer. The farm family's waiting to meet their guest of honor. Let's make it official."

My paws curled uncertainly into her lap as I stared in doubt at the giant horses, threatening cat, leaping Labbies, big red-haired man, and girls scrambling out of their car to hurry toward me. Not even in my wildest imagination had I envisioned this scenario when I boarded the white truck mere hours earlier.

The morning that had begun with the joyous certainty that I had won the grand prize of my dream human had unexpectedly morphed into a helter-skelter, crazy cast of characters. How would I ever be able to remember all their shapes, sounds, and scents, let alone take charge of this bizarre menagerie?

My mistress lifted me carefully out of the truck, holding me up high for group inspection. As my stocky hind paws kicked in the air for traction beneath my chubby little belly, I realized the title of Corgi in Charge was going to take a bit of convincing for this audience. It was obvious that I was definitely going to have to dig deep into my inner puppy if I was to become master of my new domain.

CHAPTER
FOUR

Boundaries

From earliest puppyhood, I had been made aware of boundaries. Like it or not, they were a fact of a corgi's life. Each new day brought an increased awareness of the intricate web of rules that provided structure for me and my littermates.

Some boundaries were to be obeyed without question, while others tempted a challenge from a creative puppy, even if just a little. Some were clearly physical reminders of perimeters, such as the fence encircling the puppy pen or a warning nip on the bottom from Rosemary when our exuberance exceeded her patience. Even our caretaker got our attention with a reprimanding "NO!" when little teeth were enticed by the tendril of a backyard plant that had slipped its boundary unnoticed through our enclosure fence.

Other boundaries were unspoken, but still commanded a pup's attention. Top of the list was Rosemary's stern warning stare that could stop our devilish paws in their tracks. Equally effective was our caretaker's long index finger directed at a puppy mess that landed well off target.

As my life ventured beyond the puppy pile, I found it difficult to resist the temptation to push the edges of some boundaries. The lure of exploring my ever-expanding world was just too great for an adventurous spirit to ignore. However, it seemed the more I tested those boundaries, the more new ones popped up. By the time I was transported away from my caretaker's home, I had a well-educated grasp of the boundaries that defined my birth environment. I understood those rules and had become quite adept at playing the game.

As I scrutinized my new kingdom on the day of my arrival, it was obvious that the farm possessed an entirely different set of rules from the puppy pen. New boundaries existed around every corner, as well as in the personal agenda of each unique character. As the new guy on the farm, it was all a bit overwhelming.

In my brief life, I had learned early on that boundaries were usually created by superiors to protect or exert control over lesser members of the community. It didn't take long to understand that respect and power came from control of those boundaries. Logically, it followed that if I was to become the Corgi in Charge, it would require a clear understanding of the existing boundaries before I could effectively manipulate them to suit my personal agenda.

Throughout my early days on the farm I intentionally maintained a watchful eye, studying the interactions of all the members of my new family. Even though I was acknowledged as a cute little puppy that was obviously the apple of my new owner's eye, I had to concede that I was beginning very low on the farm totem pole, especially in the opinion of my fellow four-legged critters. But, although I may have been starting at the bottom, I didn't intend to stay there for long.

Whenever my mistress had free time she lavished me with attention, but she was often busy in the barn with the horses and her students. "When you're a big boy, you can join me in the stable," she would explain, with a pat to mollify my whimpers over being left behind. "However, until you learn the rules, it's too dangerous a place for a puppy to run loose."

While she worked in the barn, I spent sunny afternoons restrained in a large portable pen erected in the backyard beneath a shady sycamore tree. It provided a perfect observation post from which to study the established farm pecking order. As humans and animals came and went throughout the day, I began to recognize who was in charge, as well as who was subservient to whom; all of it important information if I was to rule this kingdom one day.

From my earliest observations, it was clear that the farm energy radiated from my mistress, trickling down to every human and animal member of our community. She was constantly setting boundaries for the rest of us, from directing a big wagonload of hay into the loft, to correcting the Labbies for barking at passing cars, to instructing a student on riding techniques. I didn't notice any complaints about her role as the top human, so it appeared that all the members of our kingdom readily accepted her leadership.

In my quest to become the Corgi in Charge, I first zeroed in on the easiest target to charm, who was definitely the big red-haired man. His job caused him to travel away from the farm most of the week, so few of the daily farm boundaries applied to him. Home on the weekends, he was a soft touch for a game of fetch or a long belly scratch. He always seemed to know exactly where to itch to give me maximum satisfaction.

When it came to a young corgi, he was incapable of imposing boundaries. Where I was concerned, he just couldn't bring himself to say no to a puppy who regarded him with devoted eyes, no matter how great the indiscretion. I quickly learned how to keep him smiling and the treats coming. Thus, he officially became the first farm member to acquiesce to the boundaries that I established. One down!

The women who boarded their horses at our stable were also easy marks, powerless to my special blend of corgi charisma. The long hours they spent at the barn made them eligible for extended family status. We dogs came to regard these special regulars as the "Aunties." They elevated canine tribute to a far higher standard than the daily visitors who trailered in for lessons, only to leave at the conclusion with little extra time for corgi appreciation beyond a casual ear scratch. On the other hand, the Aunties invested serious time and treats to win a permanent place in my heart.

Long before I took up residence at the farm, the Labbies had trained the Aunties to stock their tack trunks with an unlimited supply of tasty cookie treats. Even though my mistress repeatedly warned them against turning us into fat, lazy dogs by spoiling us with too many delectables, we were impossible for them to resist.

I followed the Labbies' lead and quickly detected where the treats were stashed, as well as what it took to loosen the jar tops. It wasn't long before my daily cookie tally by far trumped that of the Labbies. A coy tilt of the head combined with the tip of my tongue just barely exposed was all it took to win over even the toughest audience.

The Aunties would wink conspiratorially as they rummaged through their trunks to slip me tasty treats. "This is our little secret, OK? You're just too cute to resist. What harm can one little cookie do?"

Check off another boundary overcome by corgi cunning, as the Aunties' resolve toppled like bowling pins in front of my full load of cute.

The Labbies were another easy mark. Despite being older and far bigger than I would ever grow, they were simple, happy girls with no personal agenda except food and naps. From our first meeting, it was obvious that they were no match for corgi wit and ingenuity. Beyond an incessant craving for food, they seemed perfectly content with slimy tennis balls and an extensive collection of unrecognizable, gutted plush toys that they carried around by the remnants of mangled tails and legs.

As fellow dogs, I studied them carefully from the moment I arrived on the farm, to learn the accepted canine routine. Every morning after breakfast they would do a property walkabout. Shoulder to shoulder, thick tails wagging happily, they would inspect the entire perimeter, stopping frequently to sniff or scratch at anything out of the ordinary.

I found it odd that they never once crossed the fence line. They seemed satisfied to stay within the property boundary, despite all the adventures that tempted from the surrounding countryside. Several times I ventured curiously beneath the fence without experiencing any physical deterrent. However, the moment my mistress realized I was AWOL, she abruptly recalled me in a tone that didn't leave room to disobey.

After each foiled escape, I trotted reluctantly back to her side, wondering what all the fuss was about. I noticed the Labbies were always watching from the sidelines, shaking their heads at my misdirected adventure. Whenever I questioned their reaction, they simply warned me, without explanation, "You're not supposed to cross the fence. It's just not done."

I couldn't imagine what there was about the fence that had them so worried. It certainly appeared to be a boundary that was an easy mark for a corgi—or even a Labbie, for that matter—I thought, as I waited for my next opportunity to venture off the farm.

The horses represented a boundary of an entirely different consideration. We dogs regarded them as nothing more than oversized hay burners. On the other hand, they made it crystal clear from my first introduction that none of them were particularly fond of dogs. No opportunity was lost driving that message home. Stomping hooves and large gnashing teeth posed a real threat to any errant canine that happened to stray into their pastures. It only took one narrow backside miss from a full set of snapping teeth to earn my respect for their boundaries.

I quickly learned that pasture fences represented boundaries to be respected, with no shortcuts allowed whenever the hay burners were in residence.

There existed an unspoken agreement between equine and canine to grudgingly coexist as long as we dogs remained on our allotted side of pasture fences and stalls. I was willing to accept that boundary without question, as there was nothing about those hay burners that tempted me to try to establish corgi control.

However, there was one positive aspect of the hay burners that attracted my attention. It centered on the matter of the grain that dribbled sloppily from their mouths at feeding times. I quickly learned from watching the Labbies that this was definitely a tasty addition to our barn menu.

As soon as the horses were grained, I would position myself in the aisle directly under the stall feeder opening of the messiest eater. As grain dribbled out of the slobbering equine mouth, I had only to tilt my head back and open wide. The delicious sweet feed flowed like manna from horse heaven onto my waiting tongue.

Spats the cat was a no-brainer. No way, no how, was I tempted to assert corgi control over that dauntingly dangerous fur ball. She made it clear from day one that her teeth and claws could rip the head off a mouse in one swipe, not to mention the possibilities of what could be done to a corgi puppy. If I wanted to live to adulthood, I sensed it was best to defer to Spats's clearly defined superiority over any and all boundaries that existed on her turf.

The final target on my control list was my mistress. Establishing superiority over the person from whom the farm energy flowed was admittedly going to require a little extra effort. However, as it hadn't taken me long to win over my old caretaker, how much harder could it be to gain control over this new human, who was obviously smitten with me?

*My nemesis, Spats, made it very clear that
she was never to be disturbed
while taking her morning sun on the pasture fence.*

It all came to a head early on a frosty December morning at feeding time, when I pushed her boundaries a paw
too far. As a result of my repeated exploratory excursions off
the property, normal trip-to-the-barn protocol now involved
a leash, reinforced by serious words of warning when I tried
to dawdle over backyard smells.

This particular morning, my mistress was dressed in
a bulky winter jacket, thick insulated pants, and cumber-

some pack boots. She bent over to shoulder the big black barn hose that had been stored overnight in the garage to keep it from freezing. A glance at the leash hanging on the doorknob caused her to look down doubtfully at my eager face, with the cute corgi head tilt anchored firmly in place.

Did I notice a slight chink in her armor, a hint of pleading in those eyes that until now had always held mine with authoritarian resolve?

"Beamer, I don't have a free hand for the leash this morning. Just this once, can I count on you to be a good boy and stick with me all the way to the barn? It's going to be a very long, cold day, so I really need you to work with me this morning, little buddy."

Buddy, my paw. After months of tethering my free spirit to a leash, at that moment, I didn't feel an ounce of the generous pity she sought. The way I saw it, ahead loomed the promise of a glowing opportunity waiting just on the other side of the door that she struggled to open.

She turned the knob and gave the door a hard tug to free it from the frozen seal that had formed overnight. As the ice released, the door swung open to reveal sun streaming over a snowscape that had appeared as if by magic. Almost a foot of fresh snow blanketed the pastures, driveway, and buildings, all contours blending into a rolling white landscape.

An icy blast of frigid air and snow struck us head-on and drifted through the doorway. "Ugh!" she moaned. "I am so not ready for snow."

Snow? All my senses went on high alert at the new word and the frosty crystals that stuck to my nose and ear tips. Despite my mistress's despair at the winter wonderland that lay between the house and the barn, to me it promised great adventure.

I tentatively licked the cold flakes off my nose, loving the way they chilled the tip of my tongue. If I had ever had any intention of acquiescing to my mistress's entreaty to be that obedient dog of her dreams, the sensory overload of my first snowfall tossed all reason to the wind that swirled those fluffy flakes around my head.

My mistress dragged the hose through the door, laboring awkwardly into the drifts in her heavy boots. "C'mon, Beamer," she encouraged, her voice muffled by the plaid scarf that covered her face to the top of her cheeks. "Get moving, little buddy. Neither snow, nor sleet, nor cold of winter stops the appetites of those horses."

She was so intent on slogging through the drifts with the heavy hose that she failed to keep me in sight, assuming that today of all days I would obediently follow. I hesitated in the doorway, torn between the thought of those big hay burners dribbling grain from their feed boxes into my hungry belly versus the beautiful, unspoiled blanket of snow stretching as far as my eyes could see. I was certain that white canvas was waiting for this corgi to be the first to mark it with my tracks.

The call of adventure overrode any chance of expected obedience and the breakfast urges of my stomach. In that rash moment, I threw caution to the wind and made a dash for the far fence, empowered by the temptation of unfettered boundaries.

The joy of experiencing the first snow on my terms overrode any chance of expected obedience to my mistress as I made a dash for the freedom of the far fence.

I immediately realized that running in deep snow wasn't as quick or efficient as I had imagined, especially for a puppy with very short legs. My initial leap buried me headfirst into a drift with only the tip of my bottom exposed upon landing. Not to be deterred, I dug myself out and gave a second bound that tumbled me sideways, filling my ear with snow. But, after a few drunken attempts, I began to gain a sense of traction. Very quickly, I developed a rabbit-style bunny hop with head thrown back that succeeded in keeping me upright to cover the surface at a fairly good clip.

I reached the fence perimeter before my bundled-up mistress realized I wasn't obediently at her heels. "BEAMER, NO!" she cried, instantly dropping the hose and struggling to follow me across the stable yard snowdrifts. "Come back here! RIGHT NOW!"

Oblivious to her commands, I wiggled harder to squeeze under the fence. Drunk on the freedom of my escapade, I capered circles in the snow of the adjoining field. Adrenalin was coursing too strong through my veins to recognize the depth of my mistress's anger. She awkwardly climbed over the fence in pursuit, landing face-first in a heap when her boot caught the bottom rung.

"BEAMER, GET BACK HERE NOW!" she sputtered through a mouthful of snow, struggling to her feet.

As the pitch of her voice rose, so did the level of my excitement. I dashed back toward her, darting under the fence just out of reach. Retracing my original tracks, I left her behind to haul herself over the fence again.

Brimming over with the heady confidence of surmounting my biggest boundary successfully, I joyfully bunny bounced across the front yard. Ahead loomed the tempting new horizon of the road that fronted the farm. Nothing could stop me. I was free and finally in charge; the master of my domain.

Then, through my euphoria, I heard a surreal wail fill the air behind me. As the shrill scream crescendoed, I paused in mid-flight. Curious, I turned just in time to see my mistress flop over in the center of the front yard. She fell hard to the ground, arms and legs flailing in the snow.

I hesitated, wondering what had happened. Was she hurt? Was she exhausted by our run? Or, maybe this was just a new game begging for a corgi partner. Whatever the cause, her spastic gyrations and high-pitched cries were impossible to resist.

As I neared the fresh snow mound that covered most of her body, she suddenly fell silent, motionless on her back with arms and legs limply outstretched. Curious but cautious, I tentatively sniffed the tip of a gray wool glove that poked out of the snow.

At my touch, she sprang unexpectedly to life, grabbing me forcefully by the nose before I could recoil. Her grip defied escape, no matter how I squirmed or yelped.

"Gotcha!" she exclaimed in triumph. "This is absolutely the last time you are going to run off!"

And she meant it. From that day forward until the snow melted, I was never again trusted off leash for trips to and from the barn. The Labbies sagely watched the downturn of my freedom fortunes with the now familiar shake of their heads. They too had very little sympathy for me, until the day a white van lettered with *Dog Fence* pulled into the stable yard.

I watched curiously from the glass porch window as two men in *Dog Fence* labeled shirts set about marking the inside of the farm fence perimeter with little orange flags on metal sticks. Throughout the process, the Labbies lay in the stable doorway, studying their progress with an occasional sad glance in my direction.

As soon as the flags were set, my mistress snapped on my leash without a word and led me from the house to the senior man. "Here's my incorrigible corgi puppy," she said, handing him my leash. She stepped back to join the Labbies. "I'm hoping you can instill a little obedience in Beamer."

The man bent down to fit my neck with a wide blue collar that resembled the ones worn by the Labbies. It bore a heavy black box with two metal prongs that poked uncomfortably into my neck. I shook my head at the weight, trying to paw it off, but it was snapped too tight to budge.

Oblivious to my discomfort, the trainer gave me a pat and then led me toward the closest orange flag. He drew me forward, slapping the flag as he sharply exclaimed, "No!" At the same moment, I felt a sharp electric jolt from the collar prongs into my neck fur.

"YIP!" I yelped, recoiling backward from the unexpected shock until I hit the end of the leash.

The man held tight, patted my head, and proceeded toward the next flag. Despite my vehement protestations, he continued to pull me around the fence line, repeating the flag slap—"NO!"—shock drill until we had circumnavigated the entire property.

By the time we made the last turn back toward the barn, I was admittedly humbled. I noticed that my mistress and the Labbies had never budged from their observation post in the barn doorway as they watched my tortured progress around the property at the unsympathetic hands of the Dog Fence trainer. I searched their eyes for the compassion I thought I more than deserved, but it simply did not exist.

Sporting identical blue collars with black boxes, the Labbies lay side by side, regarding me with knowing wisdom. In that moment, I finally realized why their morning property patrols had never crossed the fence line. My mistress leaned against the doorway with what appeared to be the tiniest hint of satisfaction in the corner of a smile that she tried hard to hide when I looked her way. And, sitting in the shadows just behind them was Spats, watching the show with veiled eyes, casually licking her right paw one claw at a time.

The weight of their eyes was nearly as heavy as the new blue collar I sported. In those silent expressions, I realized that the "final" boundary I so cockily thought to overcome on that snowy December morning had instead resulted in a new, electrified restriction. I sighed, sensing that no matter how many boundaries I managed to triumph over, new ones would always have a way of cropping up.

The final little orange boundary flag flapped tauntingly in the breeze. *Not today*, I sighed resignedly, sitting obediently at the heels of the Dog Fence trainer while my smiling mistress came forward to retrieve me. *But maybe someday, just maybe…*

CHAPTER
FIVE

Priorities

I have learned that priorities develop along a sliding scale that fluctuates with age, experience, and need. The categories have a way of changing in direct relation to the object of desire. From the tiniest puppy, blinking through the haze of newborn eyes, to the agenda of senior dogs turning tricks for treats, to even the humans who oversee the canine environment; our days are structured by priorities.

As a wee pup, my earliest priorities could be counted on one paw. They were identical to those of my littermates: eat, play, poop, and sleep. These equally weighted priorities formed a continuous sustaining cycle of fuel, energy, elimination, and rejuvenation that rhythmically defined our earliest days.

As curiosity developed with our ever-changing bodies, focus and needs began to shift from the purely reactive mass of the puppy pile to individualized priorities. Although Rosemary's mealtime specials always remained number one for me, exploration beyond the dinner table became a growing priority. While some of my siblings were content to sleep, sun, and scratch, from the moment I could puppy waddle the length of our basement pen, I craved adventure.

Our caretaker stimulated our curiosity with a variety of plush toys and soft rubber balls tossed into the pen to feed our imaginations. My favorite was a little blue ball banded in white. After a nap or mealtime, it was the primary object of my desire. Although a plush toy could be chewed or shaken, it eventually disintegrated beneath sharp teeth and saliva. However, a ball was something to be chased, captured, and chased again. It offered an endless source of irresistible action. I was usually the first to start a game and the last puppy to poop out. At the end of the day, it wasn't unusual to find me collapsed in an exhausted pile with the little blue ball tucked protectively under my chin.

*From earliest puppyhood, play was my middle name,
born of an insatiable desire for a rousing game
of tug-of-war or ball chase.*

Once we pups graduated to outside playtime, the simplicity of my earliest priorities were redefined by the need to touch and capture all the new shapes that filled the backyard, from sunbeams to the plastic splash pool. I also delighted in honing my newfound hunting skills. Nothing experienced to date could beat the thrill of stalking a big butterfly perched on the petal of a yellow daylily. If I was stealthy enough, it never had time to flit away from my pounce, followed by the rewarding crunch of the prize. Priority defined and rewarded with a tasty snack!

As soon as I arrived at the farm, I quickly learned that adult dog priorities had a lot in common with the eat-play-poop-sleep rhythm of puppies. The Labbies were tediously predictable girls, having refined their daily priorities down to that same simple formula. Their routine rarely varied from wake-up breakfast call to fence-line-perimeter patrol on the way to poop in the pasture, culminating in a sunshine snore against the east side of the barn that they called Labrador Beach.

The Labbies were simple, predictable girls, spending the majority of their days contentedly curled yin and yang on the grassy slope beside the barn.

The girls were not easily distracted from their routine, except when it came to guarding the farm. Beyond the promise of food, it was the one time they truly came alive. Every car that passed through the gate was met by an enthusiastic Labbie dash down the drive, backed up by a full-throated duet of deep business barks. They were true woofosauruses, neck fur bristling while their barks spewed ferocity toward the encroaching vehicle. However, if the driver took a moment to look beyond their fierce outward demeanor, he would realize the show was only a mask disguising the action of big thick tails wagging happily behind.

From first meeting, I sensed I was definitely not high on the Labbies' priority list. Once they had sniffed my bottom to ascertain that the newly arrived fur-ball puppy was not of Labrador descent, I ceased to be anything but a novel distraction to their daily routine. It wasn't that they disliked me or threatened animosity; it was just that they were secure in their priorities and were certain that I was not one of them.

But, I was OK with that thinking, as I had never aspired to be a rope-toy buddy with dogs whose ho-hum persona resembled a cross between a teddy bear and a pig. No, I had set my sights on far higher priorities than pasture patrol and barn-side naps.

To be honest, my priorities did have their origins in early puppyhood. However, as I aged, eat-play-poop-sleep became a many-layered mantra subject to change with the circumstances. By obvious definition, a corgi's priorities were self-serving, focused on the achievement of personal satisfaction, be it dietary, bodily exercise, or direct physical gratification.

Like any card-carrying member of the dog union, food was always priority number one, higher ranked than even the best back scratch or ramped-up game of fetch. As I learned the language of the farm, my favorite word quickly became *cookie,* generically used around the barn for any edible treat stashed in a human pocket or tack trunk. While mealtime kibble was a predictable right, a surprise cookie was an unexpected delight. The bearer of that treat was to be quickly identified and courted with corgi charm and cunning.

Canine and hay burners alike went on high alert at the mere mention of a cookie. Our focus was immediately redirected toward the pant or jacket pocket of the human uttering that titillating word. The delicacy could be a biscuit, a jerky strip, or even one of the hard little sweet feed balls that the hay burners craved. We dogs were much less finicky than the hay burners, readily gobbling down any edible size, shape, or texture before the taste had time to settle on the tongue.

In the pursuit of cookies, I would even acquiesce to perform what we dogs regarded as stupid human tricks. Shake? Sure. Right paw up, left paw up. Give me a cookie! Lie down? No problem. Give me a cookie! Speak? Easy excuse to bark. Give me a cookie! If that was all the work required to get paid in cookies, sign me up!

Once my hunger was quenched, I could easily be won over by a good belly rub. My humans had a talent for satisfying those remote areas that defied the reach of the claws on my short little legs. If I curled up on the sofa beside my mistress, it only took a moment for her hand to stroke my back, slowly working downward to my underside as I shifted to guide those magic fingers toward the ultimate goal.

However, as much as I loved a good scratch, personal hygiene was not high on my list of priorities. The crux of the matter was my long fluffy coat that had been a curse since it sprouted in all its unwanted glory in mid-puppyhood. No matter how often my mistress brushed and sprayed it with Show Sheen, it continually tangled, matted, and snarled. It was a magnet for all manner of dirt, brambles, and even dribbled sweet feed from the hay burners' mouths.

Unfortunately, my mistress's solution was regular grooming sessions, compounded by the dreaded bath in the big mudroom sink. Despite valiant protestations, my coat was deep scrubbed with bubbles until the water ran gray from mud and unrecognizable debris. Hosed off, toweled down, blown dry, and then snarls combed out with a little metal rake, it was an unavoidable, greatly disliked ritual. The only redeeming feature was the reward cookie offered at the culmination of the combing. But, even though I desired the treat, I made sure to initially turn up my nose, to be sure my mistress realized how put out I was.

But, if bath time was torture, a haircut was pure hell. Not even the promise of a double cookie treat made it easier to endure. My mistress figured that if she could successfully body clip the hay burners, taking off a little excess corgi hair should be simple.

With a surgeon's concentration, she set about the procedure with her handy A-8 body clippers that were easily adapted to the needs of the project. While she dipped and contorted her body to smooth out the angles of my unwieldy coat, my mistress held me helpless in a headlock. I was even flipped over on my back to assure a clean clip of long belly hair. Talk about indignities! By the end of the process, we were all miserable, and hair had invaded every conceivable surface.

Washed and coiffed, I often retreated to my private thinking space. Like every workingman in the executive hierarchy, I had the priority of a personal office. While the Labbies based themselves out in the barn, I liked to think that my office was more upscale, located in the house beside the mudroom toilet. When not on duty with my mistress, I could be found dozing between the cool porcelain bowl and the clear plastic sheet she had affixed to the wall to protect the blue paint from my frequently dirty coat.

First-time visitors to the mudroom were usually surprised to find me curled at my "desk." Without moving, I had mastered the subtle upward roll of my eyes as they entered my office. The effect caused more than one visitor to hesitate before dropping his trousers to utilize the facilities beside my head. My cunning tactics even resulted in one man retreating the moment he saw my eyes rotate upward toward his partially unzipped fly. The legend that grew from that day earned me the honorary title of Jaws of Death for the possibility of what could be.

*During off-duty times, I could be found in
my private think tank, curled up against
the cool porcelain bowl in
my executive office.*

High on my list of priorities was the weekly bank run. My mistress never failed to invite me to hop up on the passenger seat of the truck whenever she ran errands. I proudly rode shotgun, sure to shoot a knowing glance back at the Labbies sitting side by side in front of the stable, watching us drive out the gate. Paws balanced on the armrest, I would poke my nose out the window, loving the rush of air through my coat.

For my entertainment, my mistress always made her deposits at the bank's drive-up window. It only took a few trips for me to win over the teller who appeared at the window to handle our transaction. A perfectly positioned corgi head tilt combined with a cunning smile was all that was required to make her mine. Magically, a choice biscuit always appeared on the tray when she slid it out to receive our deposit. Just as magically, another biscuit was delivered with the receipt. What a perfectly wonderful financial system!

No daily priority list would be complete without a game of ball. We dogs had accumulated quite a collection of toys that were gifts from our personal humans and frequent farm visitors. There were tennis balls, whiffle balls, rubber balls of all sizes and inflation, with even a few Frisbees tossed in for variety. My favorite by far was a blue rubber Jolly Ball with a mouth-sized handle on top that made it perfect for snatching on the run and carrying back to the kicker.

There was a trick to engaging humans in a quality game of ball; a trick which I quickly realized the Labbies had failed to master. In their version of the game, the girls would will-ingly retrieve the thrown object, only to run circles around the tossing human, taunting them to try and get the ball back.

Incredible! I could only shake my head in disbelief at their antics. Foolish Labbies. Didn't they realize that humans tired quickly, becoming bored with games that required too much exertion on their part? It only took a few unrewarded tosses for their focus to drift to other activities, leaving the Labbie standing alone in the drive, holding a pointless ball in her mouth.

Determined not to repeat their mistake, early on I retrained those same humans to play the game of ball on corgi terms. Why on earth would I want to keep the ball away from them, when the sole purpose of fetch was to satisfy my passion for play? It wasn't important to me whether or not they ran as part of the game. As far as I was concerned, they could play their role quite adequately while sitting on a hay bale in the shade of the barn doorway.

I had my humans engaged from the first moment I dropped my Jolly Ball at their feet. Assuming a slight crouch, I would gaze expectantly between them and the ball, wear-ing an irresistible corgi smile of encouragement to make sure they knew what to do. The moment eye contact was made, they were hooked and the game was on. The farther they tossed it, the faster I brought it back; dropping it right on their feet so there could be no confusion about what they were to do next.

Woe be unto any sneaky Labbie who tried to intercept the ball while my game was in session. Although they were physically much bigger than me, I had no problem holding my own against them. Standing fourteen inches tall at the shoulder, thirty inches long, and weighing in at a sturdy thirty-four pounds, I was far quicker off the line. I was also in possession of sharp little teeth that I wasn't shy about using. A few warning nips on those tender floppy ears was all it took to squash any Labbie desire to intrude on my game turf. They quickly backed off, learning it was both easier and safer to watch from the grassy barn slope than to try to steal my action.

The final priority of my perfect day scenario was always well-deserved sleep. When darkness descended over the farm, and my humans were tucked away beneath a thick quilt in their four-poster bed, I curled up on my designated spot, which was a little latched rug in their bedroom doorway. Head on paws, listening as the night rhythms enveloped the farm, the Corgi in Charge was always the last to drift off to sleep on dreams filled with the new round of cookies and balls that awaited with the morning sunrise.

CHAPTER
SIX

Coach's Corner

The farm was a busy place, brimming with energy and in a constant state of motion. Coming from the quiet confines of my original caretaker's home, where a rare afternoon visitor to inspect us pups was a major event, it took me a while to adjust. From the seven a.m. breakfast feeding until the ten p.m. final stall check, the property hummed with a whirlwind of activity.

Throughout the day, cars and trucks pulling horse trailers passed through the gate, delivering an endless stream of students and training horses, as well as feed and farm supplies. Everyone who rolled into the stable yard was greeted by the official Labbie-corgi welcoming committee. The sheer volume of the girls' deep woofs overwhelmed anything I could throw out there. But, not to be outdone, while they were strutting their stuff in the driveway, I always managed to slip up to offer visitors the first personal paw in greeting.

Each new arrival came with an intriguing assortment of tires and equipment that had to pass sniffing muster. Once the humans stepped out of their vehicles, a quick nose check of shoes and pant legs identified welcome friends or put us on the alert for unknowns.

I quickly realized that, even for the super resources of a Corgi in Charge, such a busy farm made it impossible for me to be everywhere at once. That being the case, I focused on situating myself in the most important location, which was usually at my mistress's side. She was the primary source of the action, whether it was teaching, riding, or dealing with the myriad of unexpected farm problems that cropped up during the course of a day. I was certain she had a little corgi buried deep within her gene pool to maintain that nonstop pace.

The majority of my mistress's day was spent in the arena, teaching students or training the farm's horses. During lessons, she coached from a corner stool while riders performed precise exercises of her design. As her second in command, I stationed myself at her feet, always certain to put my best paw forward for the clientele.

*I took my assistant coaching
duties very seriously, stationing
myself at my mistress's side during lessons.*

During those many hours of instruction, I learned far
more about dressage than most corgis could ever contemplate
in a lifetime. Half pass, shoulder in, piaffe—I soon recognized
them all by name as well as movement. In fact, I became so well
versed on the topic that if my mistress had been forced to take
a sick day, I think I could have barked out instructions in her
absence, nipping at errant hoofs to keep the exercises on track
with the proper amount of bend and engagement.

My corner assistant coaching duties weren't limited to the students' lessons. During my mistress's training rides, I would position myself at ringside, sending out positive corgi mojo while she rode buoyant youngsters and longtime partners. Two bushy Bradford pear trees framed a wooden viewing platform that offered a nice shady post for humans and canines alike from which to observe the arena action.

My mistress seemed to welcome my presence, albeit with a few strict dog rules that left no room for compromise. Of primary importance, there was to be absolutely no barking or running into the riding ring when horses were working. It was a particularly hard rule for me to obey on those rare occasions that a youngster became fractious and bolted. Those bucking sprees fired up my corgi herding instincts, enticing me to head off the errant hay burner that posed a threat to my mistress.

The first time my hair-trigger reactions caused me to try and intercept a bucking horse, the sight of my charging paws made the youngster spin and bolt even harder in the opposite direction. He nearly dumped my mistress, leaving her hanging around his neck in a precarious position. When she finally managed to bring him to a stop, she directed the full fury of her wrath at me. Puzzled by how my usually good instincts could have gone so awry, I slunk out of the ring on the sting of her threats, wondering why it was me that was so in the wrong instead of the disobedient hay burner that had nearly tossed her.

After that incident, my mistress made it expressly clear that her rules left no room for negotiation. If I couldn't remain still outside the ring, then I would have to be locked up in the office or house whenever she rode. However, if I could quietly keep my place under the pear trees, obedience would be rewarded with cookies tossed from her pocket when she trotted past my post.

Occasionally, the Labbies would drift by the outdoor arena on one of their many daily farm patrols, but any work concerning the hay burners was of little interest to them. Shoulder to shoulder, they would pause at ringside just long enough for our mistress to toss them a cookie. Responding with a grateful tail wag, they would trot on their way to sniff out property business that they considered far more important than half passes or pirouette technique.

To my delight, corgi coaching duties weren't limited to the farm. Early in my first spring , I was introduced to the show season. Easily assuming the mantle of team mascot, it quickly became my very favorite time of year. In a farm group effort, we'd pack up the trailer with the hay burners, feed, and equipment, and then hit the open road. During the season, we followed a busy schedule, attending competitions near and far, from half an hour down the road to a full day's drive.

*Road trips to horse shows were a
special treat, where I was proud to have
the important job of riding up front
to oversee the travel action.*

When I rode in the back of our extended cab truck, the
seat was dropped down to make a flat platform that offered
plenty of room for a rug and water bowl. On long trips, I was
often allowed to slip up front between the captain's chairs
and curl in my mistress's lap when she rode in the passenger
seat while my master drove. It was the perfect opportunity for
an uninterrupted back rub that always had a way of turning
into a contented nap.

At the show grounds, we were met by the Aunties and
many of our farm regulars who trailered in their horses to
join our stabling string. Although the weekends were filled

with the pressure of competition for the riders, it was always a festive atmosphere for me. In addition to brushes and equipment, show trunks were sure to contain an assortment of yummy treats, the likes of which I rarely tasted at home. Shows were also a great opportunity for corgi spoiling, as all turned to their official mascot for entertainment and stress relief to fill the downtime between classes.

Housing on the road was an extra bonus. While the hay burners had to trade in their comfy home stalls with Dutch doors for cramped quarters, often under stuffy tents, I was delighted to discover that our horse trailer had air-conditioned living quarters. Certainly not the biggest space, but it offered all the comforts of home on a smaller scale. It made for a welcome private cool off from the summer's heat as well as a comfy hideaway at the end of a long day. There was even a perfect space beneath the pop-up table that turned into a cozy corgi cave at bedtime.

When the weather was good, my master and mistress would extend the striped trailer awning and invite the clients to join us for a family-style cookout in the evening, after classes were completed. Everyone brought a chair and sat in a congenial circle, taking turns tossing my ball until dinner was grilled. Talk about delicious corgi fare that wasn't on the menu at home! As the team mascot, it was only right that I should be treated with a sample from everyone's plate. To suit the occasion, my mistress's strict home rule about spoiling me with food was bent just a little. In my opinion, I definitely deserved those extra treats as payment for the special morale-lifting services I provided throughout the show.

At my first show, I was amazed to see how many competitors were attached to a dog on the end of a leash. It seemed that every stable group had at least one in tow. They came in all shapes and sizes, far more than I had ever imagined existed. From pouffy little white floor mops to lanky deerhounds to hairy half-breeds, they added real canine character to the bustle of the show grounds.

I was especially delighted to discover other corgis at the shows. It was the first time I had come across similar kin since leaving Rosemary and my littermates. Having been sequestered with only the Labbies for company for the past nine months, it was a relief to realize that more of my kind existed out in the world. Unfortunately, our socialization was limited to little more than brief nose and butt sniff exchanges on busy show days. Although time and circumstance didn't allow the development of deep friendships, we all recognized that under the fur we shared a common brotherhood that set us apart from mere canine.

I couldn't help but look down my nose at some of the other dog breeds that seemed from their demeanor to be little more than common stock. It was hard to believe that owners enjoyed the company of those insufferable dogs that strained against leashes, whined unhappily when left in stalls, or rudely lifted their legs on hay bales and tack boxes that didn't belong to them. Especially annoying were those feisty little Jack Russell terriers that chased rocks and yapped incessantly like they owned the place. As long as those canine reprobates stayed clear of our stable area and campsite, I served notice on their ineptitude by looking away whenever they passed.

When my mistress wasn't riding, her time was spent at ringside, coaching students in preparation for classes. I was proud that she usually kept me at her side when in teaching mode rather than shutting me away in a stall, like many trainers did with their lesser dogs. Without being too obvious, whenever I had a chance I would check out the other lucky dogs that had been allowed to join the action at the schooling ring. I noticed with satisfaction that not even the other corgis sat as straight or attentive at their mistress's side as I did.

It didn't take many public outings for me to build a genuine fan club of people who sought me out by name at the shows. My silky coat was always buffed and fluffed for the occasion; it and my demeanor made for a double whammy attention grabber at ringside. Friends and strangers alike frequently paused in passing to praise "Such a cute little man," or "He's just adorable, and so obedient," or best of all to my ears, "I've never seen a corgi with such a beautiful coat."

"He's called a fluffy," my mistress would always proudly explain. "It's a rare coat trait. Everyone who meets him loves it. When I was searching for a puppy, I was so lucky to find him with his wonderful coat."

I was rocked back on my paws the first time I heard her describe my appearance to a new fan. Suddenly, the accursed coat flaw that had threatened my young puppy dreams had evolved into a desirable trait that was so evident in my mistress's pride. From that day on, this corgi walked a little taller, never failing to give a casual toss of that special fluff to my admiring fans.

Of all my attributes, I was proudest of my ability to deliver corgi mojo when my mistress needed it most in the competition arena. Maybe the good vibes I sent her way stemmed from the luck that the woodland fairy warriors had long ago bestowed upon my Welsh ancestors as they rode into battle. I had never forgotten the legend that Rosemary had shared with us as wee pups. She had reminded us that due to our heritage we had been blessed from birth with special lucky charms, which I was now more than happy to bestow upon my mistress.

The first show I attended, my mistress spontaneously gave my head a special rub and then kissed each of my ear tips just before mounting to ride a test that had always given her difficulty. At the conclusion of the ride, she left the ring beaming, having finally achieved a flawless performance. Much to her amazement, at the end of that big class, she was announced the winner, beating competitors who had trumped her until that day.

After the winning announcement came over the PA system, she picked me up in a big delighted hug. "What a lucky charm you are! I'd like to say that special victory was all due to good riding, but I have a feeling there was something more to it."

From that day forward, a competition ritual was begun. Just before every ride, my mistress would rub my head and kiss my ear tips prior to mounting her horse. Our farm entourage, with me in the lead, would follow her up to the competition ring. I would be situated in full view of the ring, sitting quietly at attention as she cantered her big bay gelding down the centerline to an ever-growing string of victories.

No doubt about it; the abundance of treats and games provided at horse shows would be enough to satisfy most dogs' appetites, but not this corgi. I proudly sensed that I had a much bigger role to play than the average dog on show weekends. Call it coincidence, call it luck, call it superstition, but perhaps there really was a little ancient magic in the fluffy tips of my coaching corgi ears.

CHAPTER SEVEN

Pit Crew

Although my mistress seemed to possess boundless energy, I was certain she would be the first to admit that it was impossible for one person to address all the daily work the farm required. Despite the best-laid plans, the inescapable specter of Murphy's Law dictated that unforeseen surprises or problems had an uncanny way of cropping up when least expected. The knack of maintaining the expected as well as diverting the unexpected necessitated a supporting barn pit crew comprised of a variety of attending professionals, along with a full cast of worker bees.

While it took me some time to sort out all the diverse human jobs, the roles played by the farm's four-legged crew were easy to figure out. In typical "waste no energy" Labbie fashion, when the girls were not out on patrol, they were content to be passive observers camped out under the shade of the backyard sycamore or sprawled across their big pouffy pillow outside the barn office. An incoming vehicle might necessitate a brief woofing stint and an offered paw for a treat, but then it was back to nap status. Spats tended to make herself scarce whenever people filled the barn, preferring not to muddy her paws with mundane human contact. The hay burners arrogantly held themselves above all of us "lesser" furry creatures and most of the humans. In their opinion, the pit crew should always put the needs of one-toed herbivores above those of four-toed carnivores.

As Corgi in Charge, I was proud to assume the mantle of responsibility to make initial animal contact with all humans who passed through our gate. From my earliest days on the farm, I had eagerly stepped up to the challenge, sensing that this very important job had been bred into the genes of all the generations of farm-managing corgis who had come before me. However, despite my enthusiasm, it took some study to ascertain the significance of each of the characters who comprised our farm pit crew. Not only did I have to welcome and manage their activities, but more importantly, they had to be trained in the fine art of culinary tribute to be paid to the canine in charge.

To simplify the process of corgi control, I prioritized the farm's pit crew into three distinct categories, ranked by the importance of their roles, with extra bonus points thrown in for cookie production. Pit crew members considered professionals comprised the top tier. From my ground-level perspective, they tended to dress and smell better than most lower-tier members. Except in cases of emergency, their visits were sporadic, with a specific function that usually catered to those supercilious four-legged hay burners.

Topping the professional list was the vet. Doc was an agreeable man who always dressed in a khaki jumpsuit and green Wellies. The main drawback was his eau d' alcohol cologne scented with a hint of DMSO that always curled my nose. Whenever his clinic on wheels pulled into the stable yard, all four-legged farm members retreated as far as possible. Even the Labbies curtailed their greeting woofs since his visits usually contained needles, tubes, and other barbaric treatment tools.

Although Doc's visits were primarily directed toward the hay burners, even we dogs and Spats weren't immune to his services, as he was responsible for our annual shots and any basic care that didn't require a clinic visit. At the familiar sound of his tires on the drive, we could run, but we couldn't hide from the inevitable exams. But ultimately, he wasn't such a bad guy, and our shot prick yelps were quickly pacified by the bone-shaped cookie rewards stashed in his right front pocket.

In direct opposition to Doc's visits was the animal populace's positive reaction to the arrival of massage therapist. I was initially amazed by the total reversal of the hay burners' usually reticent response to visitors. On massage days, they would stand at their door fronts, big hoofs banging impatiently against the boards, demanding to be the first to be treated. If I hadn't seen it myself, I would never have believed how mellow and dreamy their eyes turned when the therapist's hands started to knead their topline muscles.

I couldn't imagine what strong magic her fingertips possessed to turn the hay burners' fractious temperaments to butter, until the morning I limped into the barn during one of her monthly visits. For several days, I had been favoring a sore knee that had been strained in a wild game of Frisbee with my humans. Noticing my uneven gait, the massage therapist dropped down beside me. After a brief exam, she suggested to my mistress that I would benefit from a treatment.

Initially, as her fingers gently probed the sore joint, I tried to pull away, dreading the pain that I was certain would follow. However, as she slowly and carefully kneaded around the injury, I felt surprising relief when the spasms in the tight surrounding tendons begin to release. That would have been enough to immediately endear her to me, but then her fingers continued to work beyond the knee, massaging shoulders and back until they finally found the nether reaches of my hindquarters.

Ecstasy; pure, complete ecstasy. I was over the moon at her touch, certain that my little legs would collapse right out from under me in response to the sensation that was far more delicious than the best pocket cookie. Mark my words, after that initial treatment I was always the first farm member waiting in the driveway to greet those magic fingers.

The final professional member of our farm pit crew was Tom, the farrier. From a canine perspective, he was a most welcome frequent visitor. Every other Thursday, he would park his traveling forge in front of the barn while he trimmed and reshod the hay burners.

The by-product of his labors represented decadent delicacies that far exceeded any other treats provided by humans. As he pared and trimmed off delectable morsels of tasty hoof, the Labbies and I would hover hungrily nearby, darting in to the work stall to snarf them up as soon as they hit the floor. No prepackaged, store-bought products for us on shoeing day. Compliments of that short, stocky man in the leather apron, we got our succulent treats fresh off the hoof. It gave a whole new meaning to belly up to the bar!

The only drawback for me in this culinary escapade was the unavoidable regurgitation that occurred without fail later the same evening. The Labbies, with their cast-iron stomachs, seemed immune to the pitfalls of overeating hoof trimmings. I, on the other hand, being a superior canine possessed of a more refined constitution, always paid a heavy price for my hoof indulgences.

What only hours earlier had been dietary manna morphed into gastric enemy number one. Without fail, my stomach violently rejected every prize morsel of those par-tially digested hoof chunks. I was left reeling with that "I can't believe I ate the whole thing" feeling.

However, once complete clearance was accomplished, it didn't take long for the discomfort to subside. In no time at all, those bi-weekly twinges of anticipation ramped up just as strong over the prospect of the next appearance of Tom's truck, bringing with it the irresistible promise of fresh hoof delicacies.

The second pit crew category was comprised of the worker bees. They were a mixed assortment of personalities who filled several part-time positions, and were responsible for daily barn maintenance and basic care of the hay burn-ers. I often felt like the stable had a revolving door through which the worker bees flew, as it seemed many of them rotated through the positions without any thought to making a long-term commitment.

They arrived for work in a variety of vehicles from pickup trucks to beater compacts, to parents' minivans, and even bicycles pedaled from nearby homes. No one criterion described the typical applicant. They could be teenagers, housewives, retired teachers, students, or unemployed work-ers floating between jobs. The one common denominator they all shared was a love of horses. Although few came to the farm with extensive prior experience, as long as they were eager to learn, comfortable handling the hay burners, and fit enough for the physical demands of the job, my mistress was willing to give them a try. Unfortunately, about the time they had mastered the position that revolving door took a turn, spinning them back down the road chasing their dreams in another direction.

At the interview, every applicant seemed to have a compelling reason to want the job. Some came in search of fulfillment of a childhood fantasy. Some came with a horse in tow, hoping to work off board and lessons. Some came just for the opportunity to be around horses. Others came as working students, exchanging sweat equity for lessons and the chance to ride my mistress's schoolmasters.

Some stepped up to the challenge, eagerly absorbing all aspects of the job. They were the worker bees who stayed the longest, grateful to expand the wealth of their personal knowledge and experience. Others were content to just put in their time, never taking away more than a weekly paycheck, even though the possibility to absorb so much learning existed. Those that refused to be challenged were the ones that came and went so quickly you could almost hear the revolving door smack them in the bottom as they headed back down the drive, disenchanted by a job that didn't measure up to their fantasy.

But, no matter what their job motivation or inspiration, with few exceptions they were a soft touch for the master manipulations of a corgi. From my perspective, dog cookie supplementation was the primary necessary employment credential. Once under my spell, they were forever in my power. I only had to sit in front of the stall they were cleaning or the hay burner they were grooming and flash them the hint of a corgi smile. Topped off by a slight, engaging head tilt, it never failed to break their work routine with an "Aw," sending a hand fumbling into jeans pockets that contained the cookie stash.

The final pit crew category encompassed all the transient services that catered to the farm's need. Day to day, there was no telling who would drive through the gate next. From technicians to parcel and feed deliveries, each required a special corgi touch.

On rare occasions, the Labbies and I worked in tandem for pure entertainment value. Our most amusing target was the monthly visit by the power company meter reader. We considered him fair game for a little canine harassment, as he always seemed nervous in our presence and had never once offered a cookie bribe. As the saying goes, "no pay, no play."

The farm had three electric meters: one at the entrance gate, one beside the house's back door, and one on the north barn wall next to the service door. That translated into three widely separated locations, requiring the meter reader to exit the cab of his truck three different times. We delighted in giving the poor man a run for his money as he stumbled over his own feet in haste to dash from truck to meter and back under the threat of deep Labbie woofs. Sometimes while the Labbies provided the verbal distraction, I would slip between the man and his truck, momentarily menacing his route back to safety with a well-played lip curl that he never failed to mistake for an intimidating corgi snarl.

As seriously as I always played my part, the Labbies couldn't stay in character for long. If that meter reader had only paused for a moment to look beyond the playacting woofs, he would have realized the Labbies' thick tails were thumping happily behind their business barks.

The legend of our ferocity lived on with each new meter reader who assumed the role of his predecessor. So deeply ingrained was our first impression on that initial reader that none of his replacements over the years ever questioned his read-and-run technique, leaving us the fun of playacting like tough guys one day of every month.

The Labbies and I always formed rank and came to
attention for the much-anticipated
arrival of the UPS truck.

The UPS delivery man was an entirely different story. Whenever the big brown truck rattled down the drive, we lined up in front of the barn in obedient military order to greet it. The smiling driver never stepped out of his cab without reaching into the plastic container next to his seat that was chock-full of yummy beef-basted cookies. He knew each of us by name, always pausing in his work to tousle furry heads as he slipped us our treats.

He didn't even get mad the day he drove out the farm gate, only to discover that I had stowed away in the back storage section. It had always been my habit to hop in the truck to investigate interesting scents while the driver took our packages into the barn. Usually, the rumble of the starting engine signaled me to hop back down. However, on this particular day I got lost in a sniff over the heavenly scent emanating from a group of boxes labeled *Omaha Steaks*. The fragrance was such an aphrodisiac that I never heard the engine roar to a start or felt the truck rattle down the drive. We were a mile down the road before the driver was distracted by my scratching at one of the boxes.

"Beamer?" he exclaimed with surprise, bringing the truck to a stop on the side of the road. "Just what do you think you're doing stowing away in the back of my truck? Get your nose out of those boxes. The steaks aren't for you."

I gave the boxes a last lingering sniff and then sheepishly made my way to the front of the truck, expecting him to dole out punishment for my indiscretion. However, to my delight, he gently scooped me up on his lap so I could see out the windshield.

"Time to take you home before you're missed," he said, turning the truck around. "You might be a sneaky little food-obsessed corgi, but I couldn't ask for a better copilot."

The final member of the third-tier pit crew was gum-snapping Frank. He worked for the local mill, delivering feed and bagged wood shavings for the hay burners. Rain, snow, sleet, or sunshine, his big white truck could be counted on to roll into the stable yard at nine a.m. sharp every Monday.

Frank was a wiry, mustachioed man who always wore a faded blue 1998 World Series baseball cap pushed back from his balding forehead. He spoke with a drawl that happily rolled out my name in high-pitched slow motion as soon as I trotted up to his truck in greeting.

Frank was definitely one to be met with joy and respect. Beyond refilling the depleted feed bin with bulging sacks of grain, he also replenished the dog and cat food containers, as well as the stash of cookie treats kept on my mistress's desk. By virtue of gastric services performed, Frank had earned the place of distinction at the top of the pit crew pecking order.

At the end of the day, I never ceased to be amazed by how many pit crew spokes it actually took to keep the wheel of our farm turning efficiently. Even more remarkable was that I was the lucky corgi at the hub, charged with overseeing it all. I couldn't help but wish my mother, Rosemary, could see the responsibilities shouldered by her little corgi son on his way to overcoming the curse of the fluffy.

CHAPTER
EIGHT

Intuition

It was no secret on the farm that a line was drawn in the sand demarcating long-established boundaries that existed between the hay burners and the canine population. Gazing arrogantly down upon us from their lofty altitude, the hay burners made it clear in no uncertain terms that we dogs were of a lower class, and unwelcome in their personal domain, which included all pastures and stalls. On the other hand, from our perspective, we dogs couldn't comprehend what qualities set the hay burners apart to deserve the pampered level of attention to which they had been elevated by our mistress.

By necessity, it was grudgingly agreed that some neutral territory must be shared. This demilitarized zone included the barn aisle, driveway, and lane leading to the outdoor arena. However, any dog caught straying into a pasture during hay burner turnout time could expect to be soundly chased from the enclosure by striking hooves and snapping teeth. It was a lesson that only took the warning of one very near miss for me to learn. Even the tempting shortcut across the side field that provided the quickest access to the house could be resisted, particularly if it was occupied by a certain overly aggressive chestnut gelding that delighted in flaunting his superiority.

Although I had learned to outwardly respect the menace of the hay burners, I couldn't resist retaliating with a little passive-aggressive response as soon as their backs were turned after they had been returned their stalls by the pit crew. It was a priceless plan that even received two enthusiastic paws-up from the Labbies.

Selecting the turnout field of the day's rudest offender, I would luxuriate in depositing a large fecal calling card on the choicest patch of clover. While a poop in the offender's empty stall was invariably cause for a reprimand from the discovering pit crew member, a poop in the pasture was a brilliant bit of business that never failed to make its point. I would be certain that it was perfectly positioned, impossible to miss.

The following morning, when the targeted hay burner was turned out in the field, I would station myself in the backyard, watching as he took his usual bucking lap of the pasture. Muscles sufficiently loosened up, he would stop at his favorite grazing spot. Stretching his neck down, salivating for that first delectable mouthful of inviting clover, he would take a huge bite, then…touché, Monsieur Hay Burner!

While the rules of engagement were expressly clear between the canine and hay burner camps, there was one horse who managed to win a place deep in my heart. If ever a corgi could have an equine soul mate, it would have been Rasir.

Although I was never a big fan of the hay burners, Rasir was a special exception with a place in my heart from the day of his arrival.

I had only been in residence at the farm for six months when he arrived from Sweden. As my mistress and I waited in the stable yard in the early dawn hours, he was led off a big commercial transport by a burly groom. Even though he was a mature horse with an impressive show record, he paused at the top of the ramp with the unsteady nerves of an inexperienced colt. Taking in his new surroundings by the dim illumination of the barn's vapor light, he blinked uncertainly.

Despite his powerful frame, I couldn't help but notice that he appeared hesitant, even a bit scared. At that moment he hooked my heart, reminding me exactly of the doubt I had felt when I first beheld my new home.

I watched as Rasir nervously searched the unfamiliar faces waiting to receive him at the base of the ramp. His big eyes finally settled on mine, drawing me in with a confused, beseeching plea. Although I knew my mistress would attend him with the same special care she showered on all the hay burners, it was obvious he badly needed someone from the farm's four-legged population to teach him the ropes.

I never knew why he picked me, but as our friendship grew over the years, I had to agree it just felt right. From that first day, I devoted myself to serving as his mascot and confidence booster, at home as well as on the road at shows. At times of stress, if he could just catch sight of me, I could tell his tension meter immediately dropped to a bearable level, no matter how great his anxiety.

He was not like the other hay burners. Although they all seemed to like him and welcomed his arrival, they were never able to coerce him into regarding us dogs with the disdain we had come to expect from the herd. Whenever I was beside him, he would stretch down to gently wiggle his big nose in the fluffy fur at the base of my neck, with the same pleasure as exchanging a companionable wither scratch across the pasture fence with another hay burner. I was proud to admit that this all-around good guy was my best friend.

My afternoon naps were known to be serious business, not to be interrupted without just cause. On one particular summer afternoon, I had staked out the perfect spot in a shady corner of the screened porch that was cooled by a soft breeze and protected from the annoying buzz of the barn flies. It also provided ideal sight lines from which to monitor the comings and goings in the barn, in case the services of the Corgi in Charge were required.

Normally the only thing to disrupt my naptime dreams was the annoyance of the Labbies' inconsequential barks at passing cars or a call from my mistress requesting a command performance in the barn. However, on this afternoon, I awoke unprovoked with an uneasy start. A sense of unexplained dread swept over me that something was very, very wrong.

Jumping to my paws, I checked around without noticing anything out of the ordinary. From the porch window, I recognized a client's car parked in front of the barn. I suspected my mistress was in the indoor arena teaching a lesson. As usual, the Labbies were draped across each other in deep slumber beside the barn. All in my kingdom appeared to be in order, yet I couldn't shake the feeling of unrest that knotted my stomach.

Call it intuition, or a sixth sense, but legend has it that we corgis are blessed with a special gift that lets us see the light of a problem while others are often still struggling to find the switch. It's a mysterious, special gift that my mother, Rosemary, said was bestowed upon us by our ancestors. Legend said we had received the gift long, long ago from the fairy warriors who had cared for their beloved corgis deep in the Welsh hills.

Whenever this special intuition came over me, I learned never to ignore it, as something of importance was sure to be in the wind. It was hard to describe the sensation other than all my senses suddenly jumped to high alert. Everything felt keener, sharper, clearer, drawing me toward an unknown action yet to be revealed.

Now filled with a growing sense of unexplained dread, I knew returning to my nap was not an option. There was nothing to do but head down to the barn for a firsthand check of the situation. Giving the sliding screen door an opening shove with my nose, I was on my way at a quick trot.

As I rounded the aisle door, everything in the barn appeared to be in order. I could hear my mistress's clear voice calmly instructing her student to lengthen stride across the diagonal of the ring. The radio softly played relaxing baroque music. The one remaining worker bee was cleaning the last of the morning tack. Some of the hay burners were nibbling the remains of lunchtime hay while others snoozed, heads bobbing dreamily out their Dutch doors.

Then, without warning, the peace was rocked by an explosive kick, followed by a resounding body slam against the wall of the second-to-last stall. Rasir! I was off like a shot toward the noise, anxious to see what was up with my good friend.

I yipped insistently in front of the stall to attract his attention. At the sound of my voice, he swung his big head around. Shaking off the fresh shavings that were stuck in his mane, he peered beseechingly at me. There was a hint of pleading distress in his eyes as they met mine.

"Beamer," my mistress called from the ring, interrupting my examination. "Come here, little buddy. I've got a cookie for you."

Even though the promise of a cookie was usually a no-brainer guaranteed to illicit an immediate response from me, for once I hesitated. I looked hard at my friend, trying to determine the cause of his distress. He bobbed his head out the open half door of his stall and snorted.

"Beamer!" my mistress called again. "Better hurry up or I'll give your cookie to the Labbies."

Taking her threat seriously, I gave Rasir a last lingering look. To my relief, he seemed to have calmed down and was now standing quietly. Considering his improved condition, I decided it was safe to leave him and respond to my mistress's call. After all, a cookie was a cookie, especially one saved from a Labbie's chops.

Almost as soon as my mistress tousled my head and offered a tasty beef-basted biscuit, Rasir gave his stall wall another sharp kick. He pinned his ears back angrily at his neighbor. The horse recoiled with a squeal and returned a harder kick. Cookie forgotten in mid-bite, I hustled back to the aisle.

My mistress was quick to follow my lead. I pushed through her legs into the stall as soon as she opened his door. "Let's take a look to see what's bugging the big man," she suggested, beginning to check his vital signs.

At her touch, Rasir calmed down and nuzzled her shoulder. I had to admit that he didn't appear physically distressed, just a bit fussier than usual.

According to my mistress, his pulse and respiration were within normal range. Upon inspection, she noted that he had cleaned up his lunch, and there was some manure in the shavings, although not as much as most afternoons.

"It's probably just the heat," she said to the worker bee, who had joined us in the stall. "You know how irritable he can get for no reason. Let's give him a little free time in the ring to walk out his angst."

As soon as Rasir was led from his stall, he seemed to settle. He casually walked to the end of the indoor arena and hung his head over the gate, letting the breeze fluff his mane as he gazed calmly out across the field. Assured that all was now right in Rasir's world, my mistress surprised me by reaching down to sweep me up into her arms.

"Keep an eye on Rasir," she directed her helper. "I'll be back down as soon as I give Beamer a quick bath. I've been putting it off all week. His coat's a mess, and I want to get it washed before we leave for the show this weekend. I've got some free time now since that was my last lesson. Let me know if anything else seems out of the ordinary with Rasir."

I squirmed and wiggled with all the force my little legs could muster under her unrelenting grasp. *BATH?! What is she thinking? Something is very wrong with Rasir. We need to stay with him. This is no time for a dunk in the tub!*

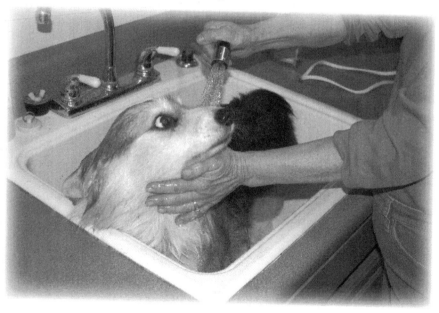

Giving my mistress a withering look, I wondered how she could ignore my keen corgi instincts that tried to tell her we should be in the barn at Rasir's side instead of soaking in the sink at this crucial moment.

But, mere human that she was, I sadly realized that my mistress didn't understand the huge mistake she was making. I was certain she attributed my agitation to her use of the B-word, rather than recognizing the real purpose of my unexpected midday barn visit. And now, I was being rudely deterred from my mission to protect and stand by my friend as she carried me up to the house to be subjected to the true insult of a dreaded bath.

No matter how I struggled or yelped in protest, there was no chance of escape from the mudroom washtub as the warm water soaked my coat. It was a good thing that my mistress didn't speak corgi, because if she had, I would have sent her on a guilt trip with an earful. In minutes I was suds up, immersed above my belly in warm water. Her restraining left hand on my neck prevented flight while the right aggressively scrubbed away the dirt embedded in every corner of my coat.

Disconsolate to have failed my friend despite my best efforts, a glimmer of escape appeared with the shouts of the worker bee who came running to the back door. " Come quick to check Rasir. He's down in the middle of the ring. He's not rolling, but he doesn't want to get up either."

Her cry for help elicited an immediate response from my mistress. In one swoop, she scooped me out of the tub dripping wet and then bolted out the door after the worker bee.

I was close on her heels, pausing only momentarily to shake out my drenched coat.

Rasir was up by the time we reached the ring. But, as soon as I saw him standing dejected, mildly pawing as though considering lying back down, I knew his condition was serious. His previously unsettled, grumpy demeanor had definitely deteriorated into a case of full-blown colic. Head lowered and ears slightly back, he watched impassively as my mistress and I approached.

"We need to get him walking," my mistress directed the pit crew girl. "I'll call the vet. You make sure he doesn't go down again while I'm on the phone."

Six hours of hand walking, two doses of Banamine, and one emergency farm call from Doc proved my original intuitive premonition correct. Through it all I was never out of eyeshot of my friend. It took teamwork to keep him moving through his discomfort. Whenever he tried to go down in pain, I would bark and nip at his heels while my mistress kept his head up and steady.

In the past, I had seen mild bouts of colic in other horses resolve with drugs and hand walking. Unfortunately, this time our best efforts failed to reverse my friend's condition. At nine thirty p.m., Doc declared that due to the growing severity of the gas distension, we could do no more at the farm. Rasir needed to be transported immediately to the veterinary hospital for surgery.

The trailer was quickly backed up to the barn door and Rasir loaded for his journey. I followed him up the ramp, stubbornly sitting down next to him in the trailer. I stared back at my mistress who stood at the base of the ramp, defying her to leave me behind. Ever since my friend's arrival from Sweden, we had shared a special bond. I had been by his side through the challenge of acclimating to a new farm and country, as well as the stress of competition and travel. There was no way I was going to be left at home when he was facing what might be the biggest hurdle of his life.

"Come, Beamer," my mistress called impatiently. "I know you want to be with Rasir, but it's not safe for you back there in case he goes down. You can ride in the truck with us. You've been his lucky charm all these years, so I wouldn't think of leaving you behind. Let's see if you can work your mojo for him one more time, when it really counts."

There wasn't much conversation on the two-hour trip to the hospital. The humans were caught up in the silent worry of what might be while I paced the backseat of the truck, sending positive vibes to my friend. Over the road noises, I knew we were all listening for any sounds from the trailer that indicated Rasir's physical distress had increased.

Our eleven thirty p.m. arrival at the hospital was greeted by a full surgical staff attired in green scrubs. I tried to jump out of the truck behind my mistress, but she gently held me back, rubbing my head to calm me. "Sorry, Beamer, but this is as far as you can go. No dogs allowed in the clinic. You've done your part for Rasir. Now you'll have to trust the humans to take it from here. Believe me, he's in the best hands for the job."

No time was wasted unloading Rasir and carefully leading him toward the hospital entrance. I was shocked by his appearance which had dramatically altered since loading up at the farm. His barrel had become hugely distended with gas, erasing any trace of ribs or hip bones. His eyes were glazed over from the painkiller Doc had administered to keep him as comfortable as possible on the trailer ride.

I frantically jumped against the window, barking encouragement as Rasir was led past the truck. He paused briefly, flicking an ear back to acknowledge that he knew I was there for him. But that was all he had to give.

I watched until the final flick of his black tail disappeared into the clinic, surrounded a swarm of vet techs and the surgeon. After all the chaotic activity of the past hours, I suddenly felt very helpless. Waiting alone in the truck, I was overcome by the frustration of having no further role to influence the outcome of my friend's ordeal.

Curling up in a ball in the center of my mistress's seat, I took small solace from the sweet scent of her perfume that had comforted me since our first meeting in my caretaker's basement. Closing my eyes, I made a silent plea to the spirit of my corgi ancestors to work their special magic. At no time more than this did I need them to watch over my friend, keeping him safe through the uncertainty of the dangerous hours that waited on the other side of the hospital door.

Overcome by exhaustion, I finally fell into a fitful sleep. The sound of the truck door opening woke me with a start, and I saw my mistress staring down at me with a faint smile. She looked ever so tired as she put her arms around me, burying her face in my neck. I could feel her tears seep into my coat.

"It's OK, Beamer," she cried softly. "Rasir made it through the surgery. We've got a long road ahead, but he's still with us. Thanks to you, little buddy, for sounding the first alarm. I should never for a moment have doubted your intuition. With a lot of care and a big dose of that special corgi mojo that you seem to have in abundance, I think he's going to be just fine."

Three hours of surgery followed by five days of hospitalized intensive care resulted in a positive prognosis that saw Rasir on his way home to us on the very appropriate Fourth of July. So much to celebrate, but no one's joy could compare with my exuberance of being reunited with my friend as he was unloaded in our stable yard and back under my watchful care.

**CHAPTER
NINE**

Party Hearty

Never let it be said that we corgis are not the supreme party animals. Ask any revelers in the know and they are certain to agree that corgis are the masters of celebration. We bring the razzle-dazzle to every shindig that makes a party not just a gathering, but a happening. Set the date, and you can be certain that a corgi will be found in the center of the action, generating merriment from his ear tips to his tail stub.

Much to my delight, our farm was never at a loss for reasons to party. Start up the grill for a barnyard cookout, raise a champagne toast on the purchase of a new horse, put out the trailer awning for a competition gathering; barn birthdays and anniversaries, Halloween pumpkins,

Thanksgiving feasts, and that granddaddy of them all, Christmas. Plan an event and I'm ever ready to lead the charge to party hearty. Game on!

True to the corgi creed to party hearty, every Halloween I masquerade au naturel as the fourth pumpkin.

My natural corgi instincts to party were awakened in early puppyhood. I remember it all began on the sunny afternoon of my litters' initial outing from the basement. Our caretaker had invited several friends for a new puppy viewing party. With Rosemary watchfully sticking close by, all five of us were gently lifted into a big box and carried up the stairs for the very first time.

Once in the backyard, our caretaker set the box on the ground, then carefully tipped it over, spilling the squirming pile of puppies onto the lawn for the great public unveiling. Rosemary was unable to contain her joy as we squinted and blinked in amazement, taking in our first rays of sunshine. She bounced with a puppy's exuberance, yelping and licking each of us from head to toe, celebrating our freedom from the basement pen.

The guests laughed with delight at our waddling, fuzzy antics as we made a first curious exploration of the tempting sights and scents of our new playground. It only took a moment for the women to join us on the grass. They squatted down to puppy level, calling and coaxing us with a gibberish mix of squeals and clicks to attract our attention. The party was on!

The afternoon passed in a blur of belly rubs, soft kisses, whispered endearments, and even tasty refreshments in the unexpected crunch of my first garden bug. It was the best of times in my brief puppy existence. But, all too soon the party ended when our caretaker declared we'd had more than enough stimulation for our first outing.

Much to our dismay, we were bundled back into the box and returned to the basement pen. But, as much as I wanted to play on, I had to admit that maybe our caretaker was right. The moment my paws hit the blanket, I fell into a deep, deep sleep. My dreams were filled with bright colors and the chirpy, happy voices of the party guests who had made a forever impression on me. When I awoke a few hours later, at the top of a sleeping pile of pups, I couldn't stop day-dreaming about when we would rejoin the yard party people for a repeat bash.

I was pleased to discover that the humans at my new farm went above and beyond expectations in satisfying my party cravings. The event could be a gala affair or as simple and spontaneous as some of the boarders hanging out on the hay bales, casually chatting after riding. I was always on the alert for those moments when no one wanted to let go of a good day at the barn and procrastinated about going home. The next thing you knew, the tops of Coke cans were popping and cheese and crackers appeared as if by magic from the house. The more they talked and snacked and the hours rolled by, the more the tasty party treats found their way down to the corgi zone.

Since the barn was the Labbies' home base, they were an unavoidable fixture at all stable gatherings. Those mistresses of mooching created some awkward moments between us, competing for the party spoils. But, I had to admire their technique; no matter how I positioned myself at the forefront of the partygoers, the Labbies always managed to reap their fair share of the goodies.

However, this was not the case when it came to parties thrown in the house. From my arrival on day one, the house had been designated as my private turf. Due to a long history of domestic damage, the Labbies were canine non grata when it came to house occupancy. The closest they ever came to an indoor visit was the mudroom. In the depths of winter, my mistress worried that the barn was too cold, even though they were bundled in fleecy coats. She would always relent to their sad faces by filling the corner of the mudroom next to the heat vent with a big pouffy dog pillow for their comfort. But, although I was forced to share my roof with them on those winter visits, their linoleum retreat was always a closed door away from party central.

One of the major highlights for me of farm party life was the noticeable absence of the hay burners. While most activities unfortunately revolved around those arrogant beasts, they were rarely included on the party guest list. The only exception was the horse purchase ceremony, where the new owner was toasted with champagne by everyone in the barn. After they had raised their glasses to the owner, the new hay burner was fed lumps of champagne-soaked sugar to welcome him to the farm family. Those brief barn ceremonies ultimately ended in my favor, when the hay burner was returned to his stall while I retreated to the house with the humans in tow to celebrate with more serious fare behind closed doors.

In my opinion as a professional party animal, there is a definite recipe for the perfect bash. Start with a generous helping of fun-loving humans; add to the mix a smorgasbord of goodies that includes a yummy assortment of meats, cheeses, and pastries; spread the menu across a variety of canine-friendly serving areas so as not to appear to be a stationary beggar; toss in a selection of toys to tug and the willing hands to pull the opposite end; and finally, when the feasting is over, season with a good scratch from the lucky guest that I have chosen to sit beside.

My all-time favorite gathering is the annual farm Christmas party held the second Saturday evening of each December. My mistress's clients and their spouses, as well as the pit crew, are invited for the biggest and best bash of the entire year.

The day begins early with me supervising the worker bee who has been enlisted to line the driveway with paper bag luminarias. Traditionally, they are lit in the evening before the first guests arrive to festively guide up them up the walk to the front door with glowing candlelight. Now, a front door entrance may not sound like a big deal to regular folks, but on a horse farm visitors tend to enter the house casually through the back mudroom door, with the front reserved for strangers or FedEx deliveries.

But, on the evening of the Christmas party, all routines are tossed to the wind on that magical night, when guests shed breeches and boots for sparkly dresses and strappy shoes that would never set foot in a barn. Even I am meticulously groomed and decked out in a special bow tie and antlers reserved just for the occasion. Doc's khaki jumpsuit and green Wellies are replaced by a navy pinstripe suit topping black shoes buffed to a high shine. Frank's stained leather shoeing apron is hung up for the evening, replaced by a red Santa sweater that lights up when he pushes a spot on the collar. Even the worker bees let down ponytails into flowing tendrils that curl softly across the shoulders of pastel sweaters.

With old farm friends and spouses coiffed and perfumed, it's a night to discover new scents, when eau de stable is replaced by exotic musk and flowery fragrances. Under normal circumstances, I can identify our farm regulars with a once-over ankle sniff, but on this night of nights all bets are off, as the unfamiliar scents drive my nose radar haywire. One sniff doesn't suffice to recognize many a guest whose appearance and aroma are drastically transformed in party mode.

When the guests begin to arrive, the front doorbell that rarely sounds throughout the year pulsates with a cheery chime. As the official greeter, each musical ring triggers a thrill of anticipation to discover who will be next to arrive. I'm off at the sound of the chime with the enthusiasm of a racehorse to be the first to greet the newest partiers when my mistress opens the door.

Upon entering the house, the first thing everyone notices is the freshly cut pine that stands in the corner of the great room, decorated in tiny white lights. Adorning the top of the tree, in place of a traditional angel or star, is a red-robed corgi figure. He wears a Santa hat and holds a long paper list of Christmas gift requests, all the while looking down upon the guests with a cunning corgi smile. Definitely my favorite ornament!

All guests arrive bearing a plate of their favorite holiday appetizers or dessert to share on a huge buffet table. Arranged between candles and holly decorations are cheeses and shrimp, dips and crackers, cookies and cakes. It's a seemingly endless spread of delicious goodies that defy even the imagination of a hungry corgi. My stomach gurgles just thinking about overdosing on all the treats.

Decked out in holiday antlers and bow tie, I am the perfect host, making the rounds of the room to welcome every party guest.

Throughout the evening, I perform my role as the perfect host. Making the rounds of the room, I am careful not to ignore a single guest. Of course, those that offer the best scratch or an extra snack slipped on the side are guaranteed to receive a little extra quality corgi time. With the room overflowing with the spirit of the season, there's never a need to sneak a treat off an unguarded plate. Even my mistress's no-snack rule is set aside for this one special evening. Let the Labbies scarf for trash can scraps in the morning, because on this night of nights I sit atop the mother lode.

Next to the food, my favorite part of the night is the carol singing. At the end of the evening, when plates are clean and appetites satisfied, everyone gathers in the great room around the corgi-topped tree. Every year my mistress rewrites traditional lyrics to well-known carols to reflect the experiences shared by all on the farm. Twists to favorite songs like "Joy to the World, He's on the Bit" or "I'm Dreaming of a Grand Prix Horse" or "Jolly Old St. Rasir" cause everyone to laugh and sing out in holiday harmony.

The pièce de résistance and the closer of the night has become everyone's traditional favorite. My first Christmas on the farm, my mistress debuted "Beamer the Corgi," sung to the tune of "Frosty the Snowman." It was an instant hit with the guests as well as me. When the time comes, my mistress never fails to call me to her side in the center of the room. When the revelers raise their voices in harmony, I join in with my best corgi yodel as they sing:

Beamer the Corgi was a jolly, happy soul
With a bunny butt and a button nose,
And two eyes made out of coal.
Beamer the Corgi was a fairy tale, they say.
He was made of hair, but the Labbies know
How he came to life one day.
There must have been some magic
In that old rope toy they found,
For when they placed it in his mouth
He began to dance around.
Oh, Beamer the Corgi was alive as he could be,
And the Labbies say he could laugh and play
Just the same as you and me.
Thumpetty thump thump, thumpetty thump thump
Look at Beamer go.
Thumpetty thump thump, thumpetty thump thump
Over the pastures so.

The chorus always ends with applause round the room and cheers of "Yea, Beamer!" and "Go, corgi!" I never tire of all the encouraging faces that smile my way, from the beaming Aunties, to the clapping worker bees, to my healer Doc and Frank the master treat supplier. Best of all is my mistress, who smiles the proudest of them all. So many special humans, all of whom have generously opened their hearts to me in their own unique ways, since the day I arrived on the farm as a mere pup.

Warmed by the embrace of their love, there is no doubt about it: I am one lucky corgi. At this special season, I'm reminded more than ever that I was definitely blessed with some amazing fairy magic the day my mistress came into my life those many years ago. All the more reason at this holiday season to let the good times roll. Party hearty!

CHAPTER
TEN

My Ancestors' Paws

The farm is my kingdom. Over the years, I have learned to rule my domain with a firm but benevolent paw. In all my actions, I have always tried to do honor to my farm family, as well as to the tradition of my ancestors that was passed down to me from Rosemary through the generations of Welsh corgis who preceded her.

Hard as it is to believe, another year of life has run full circle, culminating in the anniversary of my arrival at the farm. It seems like only yesterday that I was curled in my new mistress's lap, hesitant to exit the truck and enter the new world that awaited. I remember peering uncertainly out the window, wondering how I would ever become the Corgi in Charge of such a very foreign place that was destined to become my permanent home. But, my time on this farm has blessed me with so many special moments, so many memorable people, and so many gastronomic celebrations since that long-ago day in June which marked the start of a truly remarkable life.

Seven a.m. Peace envelops the stable with the sunrise as the music of the farm begins to tune up, setting the rhythms of the day that awaits. The demanding crescendo of the hay burners' morning hunger has finally subsided. Their snorting, stomping, and wall kicking has lulled into quiet munching with the arrival of breakfast. Feed tubs quickly licked clean, their big faces are now contentedly buried deep in flakes of sweet-smelling timothy hay.

The Labbies and I have finished the serious business of aisle sanitation, snarfing up all the dribbled grain from the floor outside the hay burners' stalls. As soon as the last scrap of feed is licked up, the girls are off on their first farm patrol of the day. Striding shoulder to shoulder, the tips of their happily waving tails are just visible against the second pasture fence. Unless an unexpected scent is uncovered that requires investigation, they will soon return to collapse in a napping pile against the sunny stable wall, until the first visitors arrive bearing the prospect of pocket cookies.

Spats has assumed her usual morning position, hovering vulture-like on the top rung of the side pasture fence. She waits, amazingly immobile, for the first mouse of the day to surface, and then the game is on, with the outcome always in her favor. Over the years, that cat and I have finally arrived at a workable, albeit tenuous, truce. The now gray-whiskered queen of the barn has definitely mellowed from the hell-on-paws feline who stalked me with contempt from the first day of my arrival. While we have grudgingly agreed to tolerate each other's presence in the barn, I readily acknowledge that as long as she prowls the aisle, she will never dance to the beat of my drum as I have trained so many others to do.

Unless we are on the road at a horse show, my mistress always personally takes charge of the morning feeding of all the furry folk in the barn. I am never more than a step away from her heels, ever ready to supervise the serving of all food products, as well as retrieving any edibles accidentally dropped. Once the morning chores are completed, my mistress returns to the house to eat her own breakfast, leaving me and the Labbies in charge of the barn. Usually her return coincides with the arrival of the worker bees, signaling the daily start of action on the farm.

However, today being the anniversary date of my arrival, I know there will be a break in the usual routine. From past experience, I am certain my mistress will soon return to the barn bearing extra cookies to mark the occasion. The treats will be for me alone; definitely not shared with any overindulged Labbies, which I'm certain will be looking on, enviously licking their drooling chops while I savor my gift. Best of all, I know I can expect a special game of ball to be played just between my mistress and me before the first hay burner is led from his stall.

*Ball games are great anytime, but on
my anniversary it is an extra-special treat between me
and my mistress that takes priority over everything,
even the hay burners.*

The anniversary date has always been the perfect time to reflect on the evolution of my life. I will never forget the uncertainty of those earliest puppy days, worrying about the unknown ramifications of being cursed with an overabundance of hair that might deter the interest of a special personal human.

Thankfully, over the years that thick fluffy coat has turned into a blessing bearing immeasurable rewards. I am forever grateful that my mistress was willing to adjust her corgi appearance expectations in her selection of me. She has proven time and time again that she could never be put off by a little surplus hair that has grown beyond the corgi norm. In fact, to my amazement, she actually seems to celebrate all the fluff.

As much as my mistress has been a blessing for every aspect of my life, I think that I, as well as the qualities of my special coat, have provided her with an equally great source of pleasure. Whenever she is stressed by the demands of the farm or a disappointing session with the hay burners, I sense that nothing seems to lower her tension level more than running her hand through my fluffy coat. At those times, she will snuggle me close in her lap just like she did when I was a pup. As she pensively runs her hands through the long silky strands of my coat, I can feel her worry fade away with each stroke.

Gradually, her fingers begins to relax until the choppy, stress-filled strokes over my back are replaced by a deep shoulder massage that's well worth the wait. It's a special release that

I'm proud to say only the two of us share. Curse of the fluffy? Bring it on! Because, I've faced down the challenge and turned that curse into a definite blessing.

My mistress has returned to the barn, tacking up her first ride of the day at the completion of our very enjoyable full-on game of kick the Jolly Ball. Feeling my paws were at their quickest on retrieval, I am proud that I have not lost an ounce of agility to the passage of time. I even sensed the Labbies were impressed by my nimbleness as they watched from the sidelines.

Anniversary celebrations completed, I assume my usual morning sentry post between the stable's Kentucky doors, still savoring the satisfying morsels of a beef-basted cookie that is lodged between my back teeth. As Corgi in Charge, I await the opening of the driveway gate, admitting the first visitor of the day for me to inspect and greet. Here I shall happily remain among family and friends, a loyal heel nipper of the Welsh fraternity, maintaining order and faithfully guarding as I proudly carry on the tradition of my ancestors' paws.

*Each morning as Corgi in Charge,
I assume my official sentry post, waiting
to welcome the first visitor of the day.*

Made in the USA
San Bernardino, CA
19 December 2016